HIDDEN EPIDEMIC

Training Helpers for Adult ACE Survivors

(Adverse Childhood Events)

Gary J. Butler, Ph.D.

Battle Press

SATELLITE BEACH, FLORIDA

HIDDEN EPIDEMIC

Training Helpers for Adult ACE Survivors

(Adverse Childhood Events)

Copyright © 2025 by Gary J. Butler.

Battle Press books may be ordered through booksellers or by contacting:

Battle Press
1-919-218-4039
steve@battlepress.media
www.battlepress.media

ISBN: 979-8-9887651-9-6 (softcover)
ISBN: 979-8-9905619-0-8 (eBook)
LCCN: 2024908820

First Edition.

Other Books by Gary Butler:

Becoming Free: Recovering from Adverse Childhood Events (ACE's): Healing from a Hidden Epidemic.

Table Of Contents

Dedication

This book is for the thousands who have been so brave in recent years through telling their stories of the impact of childhood abuses. It is also for those who will be continuing in the future to follow in their footsteps to speak about their truths of the impact of early childhood abuses, and that healing of past wounds is possible.

The author extends a heartfelt appreciation for those professionals and helpers who have walked faithfully beside survivors with compassion, non-judgmental responses and loving understanding.

There are many family members and friends who have helped make this a better publication. To name a few: my cousin Joyce Pulcini, Lance Taylor, Dorothy Godbold and Dr. Bill Greenlee.

To my loving wife Lori for her support and patience as I wrote and re-wrote this work. I extend a warm and loving thanks.

This is also to recognize the importance of the patience, inspiration and understanding of the publisher, Battle Press and the editor, Steve Gillem.

Introduction

There is a tremendous need for a step-by-step treatment program to help adult survivors heal from childhood trauma. This book presents the steps of a treatment program that guides the helper (caring friend, with a trained non-professional or a professional) to lead the survivor through the recovery experience. The helper will learn about assisting survivors in identifying and expressing their feelings, gathering together the details of what happened in the traumatic events and discovering the impact generated from these early scenes. They will also learn creative ways of being able to forgive and re-write the hurtful episodes.

I am truly excited that you have picked up this book! Your action indicates you have an interest in learning about helping survivors free themselves from the impact of adverse childhood trauma. I respect that you the reader could be a survivor in search of a program like this one. If so, the author strongly encourages you to find a trusted friend to walk with you, step by step as you go through this program. I strongly advise you to give this book to a professional to deliver the program with you. When considering utilizing this program, realize it was developed in an inpatient program with 24/7 staff available and a self-help group. It is recommended that you and your helper consider working with/through a professional.

This is a creative program utilizing imagery and specific sequences that flow seamlessly from one step to the next. There will be very little guesswork because a great majority of the tasks are spelled out like a script. All the helper needs is a desire to listen in a nonjudgmental, accepting way. All of the steps of the treatment program are offered in this guide.

One of the major motivators to be involved in this work comes from being a part of observing the survivor growing, getting his/her power and his/her life back. Another way of putting it would be from watching the survivor find his/her voice. The process gently leads survivors into personal discoveries to experience the impact of becoming free of layers of the burdens they have been carrying from being abused. One of the unique components of this program involves the discovery of one's Precious Child (PC). The steps in the program lead up to the time for the revelation of this part of oneself. This is the true self that existed before the trauma. This is the one that was whole and fully intact, before the hurtful events. This one is able to love, forgive, be curious, make mistakes, learn, and go on to be loved as well as develop one's strengths and gifts. This experience is awfully close to the experience of being present at the birth of a child or seeing a partner propose seeking his/her partner's hand in marriage. There is nothing like it.

The focus of this work is inspired by the recent discovery that the occurrences of early traumatic events are more prevalent than previously thought. The study was conducted by polling a large group who had successfully completed a weight loss program. Many who were enrolled to complete the follow-up on how to keep the weight off dropped out of the study. It was discovered that 63 percent of the participants had at least one occurrence of an adverse childhood event (ACE). The report was published in 2010 by Vincent Felitte, MD and Robert Anda, MD. It has been termed a **"Hidden Epidemic"** by the editors, Lanius, Vermetten and Pain of the book containing the study (see the Selected References at the end of this book).

Before this extensive study, it was generally thought that approximately 25 to 30 percent of people had experienced an abusive event. The study also discovered that the greater the kinds of abuse one experienced, the higher number of other issues occurred, such as suicides, participating in high-risk behaviors, drug use, early pregnancies, psychiatric diagnoses, PTSD, dropouts from society, and more. Seasoned therapists would recognize the connection between successful weight loss and the reason people dropped out of the second part of the program to keep the weight off. For many, the weight may have served as a protection or medication connected to an attempt to heal some unresolved pain from back in time or to not appear attractive.

This program parallels a program I put in place several years ago at an in-patient treatment center for adults who had suffered ACEs. To date, I have helped approximately 300 survivors. I am here to share what I have learned and assist you in achieving whatever goals you may set for yourself in this field as a lay or professional helper.

I will provide many tools to assist you in growing to any skill level you desire as an adult, lay person, professional, or non-professional. The survivors I have helped include adults with a burden from childhood, retired police officers, retired military, and first responders from all walks of life.

My goal is to establish educational centers in cities to spread the word about this hidden epidemic. Additionally, the centers would offer training classes for helpers and individual or group therapy for survivors, including self-help groups. The overall purpose for the centers will be to offer affordable relief from the impact of early traumas. This is my passion and my purpose.

I too am a survivor. For years, I had been affected by the impact as a 5-year-old from watching my father beat up a man in our home. The man had made a pass at my mother. I was 44 years old when the unmanageability caused by that early scene that had continued impacting me through the years caused me to stop and take stock. Why was I so compulsive about being the best and the fastest? Why did I incessantly work 60 to 70 hours a week seeing patients and families?

As I discovered the connections between past hurtful events and current behaviors, my life began to change for the better. I made choices to change in ways I could not have made before becoming curious about some of my behaviors. One major realization was that I worked all the time because being close and available to my family triggered a fear. So, working hard was a mask for covering the fear of being vulnerable in close relationships. My old hidden belief was that being close could kill you or in some way lead to your death. Once I made the connection to that early painful scene and its role in my life today, I could then begin to work on embracing some new assumptions about me, work and life in close relationships.

This weight loss study brought to the forefront the "Hidden Epidemic" (over 60% of the participants had at least one occurrence of an ACE), and my own story as a Survivor that provided the primary motivation for publishing this book. That is to train more people who have a passion for helping survivors become free of the impact of early traumatic events. It is to bring awareness to society in general of the prevalence and the impact of these early adverse events. You could be a licensed professional, a counselor, part of a ministry, a social worker, or even a concerned friend or family member with a desire to help. You could also be a survivor seeking recovery from the impact of adverse events in your life. I purposely remind you again that recovering survivors make great helpers.

Preface to Chapter One

Lots of people need help to heal childhood trauma and a tremendous need to train helpers (caring friend, a trained non-professional or a professional) to lead the survivor through the recovery process. Since the word, "survivor," is used so frequently, I will use the capital "S" in place of the word.

I recently reached out to a young man whom I had led through this recovery process many years ago. He was in bad shape in the beginning, but over time he has become better and better. He now has a lovely family. He said we need to have one of those "Precious Child" sessions because he currently finds himself getting frustrated with his own children who were about the age he was when his severe abuse started. He does not want to repeat what the angry males in his family did to him. The point is that recovery comes in waves. The waves may become smaller and even go away for a season or two then return again anew oftentimes with a different twist but with a similar trigger.

The work is not always completed in a course like this one. Issues can extend throughout one's life. A course like this clearly creates a foundation for one to get into a good recovery. It is the tools of recovery learned in this course that can help the S to work through new issues that may show up in the future.

So, since you have a desire to develop familiarity with a program like this, I applaud you. All the steps and activities are spelled out in detail. You will be so glad that you picked up this well-thought-out program.

This awesome program begins with setting a way of thinking and a check-in. It was developed for you and an S or group of S's you are in a position to help. Before beginning a session with an S, clear your mind so you will be receptive to whatever your S needs to say. You cannot predict what has happened to another human being at the mercy of offenders. I strongly recommend that you are familiar with self-relaxation methods. These are detailed in Appendix G.

You will be assisting the S in rewriting his or her painful memories, forgiving the offender(s), and how to take the new learnings into the future. All of these steps are detailed in this guide.

One story comes to mind about the satisfaction that comes from helping an S make sense out of his or her abusive life. This young wife and mother began to feel fear and began to withdraw from her husband, whom she loved very much. After some exploring, it was discovered that his hands reminded her of her stepfather's. Upon further inquiry, it was revealed that the stepfather had violated her sexually over a three to four-year period. She had not reported this abuse. Out of shame and the private nature of the abuse, she kept it to herself until this session. As so frequently happens, her offender threatened to hurt her and her younger brother if she told anyone. So, she kept the secret to herself all those years. She was encouraged to attend a self-help and therapy group. Her husband was a part of her recovery work, and she eventually was able to be comfortably intimate with her husband again. This is an example of how rewarding it can be to help S's become free of the impact of the early abuse.

If in the course of working through the program and the S seems tense, it's recommended to take a moment and lead them through self relaxation.

I invite you to close your eyes and imagine this scene in your mind's eye. Imagine you are walking in the woods following along a gentle path. You can hear a slight breeze moving the leaves in the trees. Beams of sunlight find their way through the branches and shine like spotlights dancing on the forest floor. You become aware of birds chirping happily and flitting about among the branches. Up ahead you can hear the sound of rushing water. As you approach, you can see the water moving swiftly around several large rocks that lead to the far bank. You become aware of the other person walking with you on this trail. The two of you agree that it would be wise to help one another across the rocks to avoid falling into the fast-moving stream. You move to the edge of the bank and stretch your leg out just enough to place your hiking boot on the first large stone. As you balance yourself on one leg, you bring the other onto the rock. As you reach out to offer your hand to the other person, place this scene on hold. Then reduce it in size and push it far enough away that it disappears. Tell yourself that you can revisit the scene in the future. Once the scene is gone, open your eyes and when you are ready, proceed on to Chapter One.

Chapter One
What Happened? Let's Get Started

*"A survivor's journey to personal freedom
begins in earnest when in the presence of
a safe listener, he or she can share the full
truth of what happened."*

—Gary J. Butler, Ph.D.

INTRODUCTION

By design, this will be a fairly short chapter. Basically, it is to get things started right where your survivor is emotionally and mentally in dealing with his/her ACE's. It is to start with something the survivor is probably wondering how he or she will do knowing at some level that he or she will have to tell his/her story.

Note: The Appendices contain the tools and forms needed to complete the steps in this treatment program. Helper, it is recommended that prior to meeting with the S, print out the forms needed to accomplish this treatment program. Copy pages from the Appendices or download the packet of forms in the Appendices using this link:

https://tinyurl.com/3rkhjpv6

A. The first task is to prepare the Helper to be there for the S and how to best assist the S to tell his or her story:

1. Helper, before asking your S to tell his or her story, clear your mind of any unnecessary thoughts and relax your body so all tension and tightness are gone. Do this right now for yourself to get your mind and body set for listening to your S. Once you have cleared your mind and your body is relaxed, tell him or her, "In a moment, I am going to ask you to share what you are aware of concerning your story. This does not have to be well thought out or presented in any particular way other than how it comes out. You can feel any feelings that come up. Relate whatever comes to mind. If you sense that not many details are available, that is understandable, and this will be remedied as you proceed through the course of the program."

2. Helper, your response is to just listen and affirm what you have heard without adding or distracting from what your S is sharing. As a helper, your safest response is just to reflect on what you heard. You could begin with "What I hear you saying is…."

3. Helper, continue by saying, "One rule I want to introduce here is that feelings are always respected as we work. We ask that you not talk while experiencing any wave of feelings. As you stop to feel your feelings, note what it is like to experience them. Then make comments about the experience after the wave has passed. This exercise is the beginning of discovering the details of what happened."

B. Preparing to ask the question about what happened.

1. Helper, you will be taught how to help the S access more details from his/her memories of abusive events

through the use of imagination and various other tools. Eventually your S will be able to answer 17 powerful questions after reviewing a scene. These answers will be recorded on a Master List of Abusive Events numbered for each painful event. (see Appendix E).

2. If you are both ready, Helper, say to your S in a calm and soft voice, "I would like to hear what happened to you. Just share what comes to mind. This is your recovery. This is your story. This is your truth. You did not cause this or these hurtful events. You were just a child. You deserved to be protected. I am ready to listen to your story. Take all the time you need. This is not a NASCAR race. You have the right to proceed at your pace. It is okay to share as things come to your mind. It does not have to be well-organized or well-thought out."

C. Helper, listen and affirm with your S as he/she relates his/her story about what happened. As you listen, decide when you would like to reflect back on what you have been hearing. You can begin with the reflective listening format, "Let me see if I am hearing you right?" You are looking for the S to affirm or correct what you have said.

D. When you sense that your S has finished for now with his/her story, thank your S for sharing his/her truth. Assure your S that he/she did great. You can say, "Thank you for sharing your truth. I am so sorry that you had to endure such painful trauma. You did not deserve such treatment. You deserved to be protected and cared for in a loving way. Let me assure you that you did a great job in honoring your truth by speaking about it."

Closing This Chapter. Once this first task seems complete, Helper, give yourself a pat on the back. You listened, affirming your S. You helped your S get off to a great start. I am sure your S is relieved to get this part behind him/her and appreciated your kind and gentle support.

Before putting this chapter to rest, I invite you to close your eyes and bring up in your mind's eye, the scene in the woods by the fast-moving stream. You are standing on the first rock with both feet planted. Now imagine reaching back to help your partner to step off the bank and step onto the first rock next to you. As you reach for his/her hand, you encourage your partner to step on the large rock with you. As you stand there together, you are aware of the first important step you have taken together to safely move across the fast-moving waters. Now, become aware of the importance of working together to stay safe. You look forward as you can see the next rock to safely step onto. With this awareness, let the scene fade away knowing you can return when you are ready to continue the journey.

Move on to Chapter Two when you are ready.

Chapter Two
Identifying and Expressing Feelings

INTRODUCTION

This chapter is about the typical issues Survivors (S's) have in recognizing and expressing feelings. Most S's have difficulty expressing feelings. Considering the abuses S's have endured, it is no surprise that dealing with their emotions can be an issue.

A. It is essential to provide some background for the Helper to have some understanding of the issues and dynamics for assisting the S in dealing with feelings. You will get an excellent set of tools to be able to assist your S.

B. Sometimes the core issue S's experience is that they only express feelings in extremes. This leaves them feeling concerned that they cannot turn them off. It is not unusual for the S to feel anxiety from being out of control. Some are therefore hesitant to feel anything out of fear they will be overwhelmed with a flood of feelings.

C. For others, it is confusing to know whether they are dealing with the past or the present. When an S experiences an intrusive memory, the S believes he or she is back in time. They can be triggered by present realities that are similar to unhealed remnants from the past. For others, they can be so overwhelmed with a deluge of intense, unexpressed feelings that all they feel is numbness.

D. Understanding the concept of going back in time requires us to talk about "triggers."

    1. Let me give you an example about how triggers work. This example comes from the treatment center where I was the Clinical Supervisor. While traveling in a 45-passenger bus transporting some of the patients to a wooded area to experience an outdoors challenge course, one of the patients fell on the floor. She flailed about as she screamed and yelled at imaginary attackers. Something had triggered her to return to an early memory.

    2. There were many triggers that were revealed in consultation with her once the group had returned to the treatment center. One of the triggers occurred when she saw fleur-de-lis on the metal fence posts lining the perimeter of the complex. Her abusive episodes were performed in a densely wooded area containing fleur-de-lis. The area for this outdoor challenge program was in a heavily wooded area. With all of these potential triggers present, her subconscious moved into a protective fight mode. She thought she was back in time. She dissociated into the old memory. Later, back at the center, she and her group could process what happened. She was experiencing extreme fear and anger at the remembrance of her offenders. To her, it was as if she was in the presence of her offenders.

E. Because this issue of sorting out feelings and the expressing of them can be extremely complex, we have to start from the simplest of tasks. We will begin by inviting you, the Helper, to assess how in touch the S is with his or her internal feeling realities.

   1. Explain to your S, "I will ask some questions. You are to complete the answer by speaking what feeling or feelings first comes to mind to the word being presented. Here are some words I will present to you. When you think of home or father, mother, work, wife/husband, your future, your childhood, friends, and the town you live in, as I say these words what feelings come up?"

   2. "Let's start with the first one. What comes to mind when you think of 'home?" (Helper, present the keywords: home, father, work…one at a time. Also allow time for the S to find and name their feelings if he or she can find any).

   3. Helper, keep repeating this exercise, giving your S time to use this system of discovering the appropriate feeling word or words. If your S seems reluctant, unskilled in finding feeling words, or even stumped, it is ok to just go on at his point.

F. The basics of dealing with feeling words: the basic eight.

Note: Reference Appendix A, "A Tool For Discovering Primary Feeling Words."

   1. If the S is unsure or hesitant, explain by saying to them, "We will start with the basic eight feeling

words from which hundreds can be derived. These eight words are: joy, sad, pain, guilt, shame, anger, fear, and lonely. We will refer to these as primary feeling words, or PFWs for short."

2. Helper, continue by saying, "Each word has a gift or purpose. **Joy** is about celebrating life. It reminds us that achieving some goal is worth it. Or it may be the happy feeling from helping a friend. **Pain** alerts us that we have a hurt that is in need of attention. **Anger** directs our attention to an impasse or frustration blocking our path to something important to us. It activates the energy to press on through difficult challenges, even to face situations that seem grossly unfair. **Sad** comes when we experience disappointment or loss. It could be what one experiences when someone you are close to dies or is badly hurt. Shame and guilt get confused frequently. **Shame** is that feeling when we have erred, but it is not behavior that would get us in trouble with authorities. Shame could come when we forgot, for example, to fulfill a commitment to attend a celebration for a friend. **Guilt** alerts us that we are about to commit (or have in fact already committed) a misdeed or crime for which the authorities could hold us accountable. **Fear** is a reminder that we need to move cautiously for there is a potential danger now or ahead. **Lonely** is an alert about how important others are to us and this feeling comes when we are by ourselves. "

G. The basic skill is to be able to go inside and discover what primary feeling word or words fit a particular time and experience.

1. Ask your S, "Think about recent experiences from the current day or events over the course of the past couple days. As you remember these certain recent events, discover what PFWs would best fit." If the S can identify the PFWs, then go on.

2. If he or she is having difficulty, then direct your S to Appendix A. This Appendix is designed for identifying PFWs from a list of descriptor words. Allow time for the S to read through this and practice using the tools presented to find PFWs.

3. Once the S has become familiar with the process, then ask the S, "Recall some recent occurrences again. As you recall some of these, use the process described in Appendix A to discover the PFWs that are a fit." Do this exercise until S is fairly competent at identifying the PFWs that are a fit.

4. Bring the S's attention to the importance of recognizing the internal experience when the feeling words selected are "right on." Say to your S, "I want to alert you to noting your unique internal experience when you have selected the correct feeling word or words. This little internal feeling is one of peace or comfort unique to you. Whatever yours is, it will tell you when you hit it right on dead center."

5. Helper, say to your S, "It is important to note the differences in what words come in the blanks in these two phrases:

'I feel_____,'

or

'I feel like_____.'"

a. Continue by explaining, "When someone says, 'I feel like _____' what follows is not a feeling. It will be a thought."

b. Ask the S, "Think about events of recent days. Use the format to complete the blanks for 'When I think of _____ I feel_____.'"

c. Now complete the blanks for 'When I think of _____ I feel like_____'"

Practice recalling a number of recent experiences while using each format, "I feel vs. I feel like."

Once this is complete, ask, "S, think about some upcoming events. Now complete the format as before, 'When I think of _____, I feel_____.' Then, use the format 'When I think of _____ I feel like_____'" Discuss how this experience comes across with your S.

Complete several of these exercises until you become confident in using this format. I encourage you to experiment with using these formats during the day to assist you in becoming familiar with distinguishing thoughts and feelings.

d. Helper, ask your S, "Repeat these two positive self-talk statements and write them down. They are to be placed on your bathroom mirror to review daily until you are willing to internalize them in actions and beliefs:

1. "My feelings are mine. They reflect the reality of my personal experience and (most importantly) they are not up for debate!"

2. "What am I feeling at this moment? How much is this feeling about my past? How much is it about what is going on right now?"

CLOSING REMARKS

Tell your S, "You did a fantastic job at getting better with identifying and speaking about thoughts as different from feelings. In this next chapter we get more into the sources of the pain. Like it or not, to get better, we have to take time to go back to face these past hurts that are unhealed. It is part of the process of getting free of the impact. I will be right beside you each step of the way. The only way through is to go on through."

CLOSING THOUGHTS FOR THE HELPER

Helper, you got a wonderful start being present for your S in both these chapters with your mind and body cleared. Your purpose is to be there for your S. I am sure that you gained a great deal from guiding your S through this segment. At this point, you will understand more about feelings and their importance than the great majority of people you encounter in your life. You have assisted your S in laying the groundwork for the remainder of the tasks ahead. Feelings are an integral part of every step in this process to recovery.

You are well on your way to building trust with your S. Being present with your focus on him or her, being available to hear his or her story without judgment and being patient while they learned about expressing feelings demonstrates that you care and are safe. Knowing you are safe is the number one skill to bring to each session.

I invite you to close your eyes as before. Bring into your mind's eye the fast-moving stream in the woods and you and your S standing on that first large rock as you prepare to step onto the second one. Imagine yourself extending your right leg out towards this second rock as you shift your weight then carefully bring your other leg securely onto this second one. With your feet firmly standing on this rock, you reach out to invite your S to begin stepping across towards you. As you reach out, you firmly grasp his/her hand. You gently secure his/her hand and move with him/her as your partner onto this second rock next to you. With both of you safely standing on the second rock, you take a moment to realize how far you have come together across this stream. You take a moment to assess how many more steps there are yet to reach the far bank. With the water rushing all around you, you both have remained dry. With that in mind, begin to let the images slowly fade away. Remind yourself that you can return to continue this journey later. Be aware of the self-confidence you and your S have been building as you are progressing across this fast-moving water.

When you are ready, clear your mind as you go on to Chapter Three.

Chapter Three
Source Of The Early Hurts

INTRODUCTION

Helper, I know you have been patient and understanding. This is great and exactly what your S seeks. To be guided by gentle hands and not be judged is wonderful for any S. They tend to soak up and treasure being accepted right where they are. This is the essence of expressing love to them. Keep up the great work of honoring feelings as well as being just what your S needs, an open, accepting and non-judgmental listener. It may not seem like a big deal to you, BUT let me assure you that it is a major deal. With each step accomplished, any resistance on the part of the S to face the painful memories will lessen. The basic task is to review and name the acts of abuse perpetrated onto your S when he/she was an innocent, vulnerable child. This sets the stage for discovering the impact.

1. Becoming familiar with the categories of abuse.

    a. Some things of which to be aware.

        (1) What the S is about to reveal is somewhat like opening a time capsule. Sometimes the material and the feelings have never been shared with another person. Your S may even be totally surprised by how strong the feelings may be.

        Helper, prepare yourself for the S being flooded with waves of feelings. When you are ready, begin this task by saying to your S, "As was stated before, we will be moving into some memories that contain a great deal of strong emotions. I encourage you to not talk as a wave of powerful emotions comes on to you. Wait until any wave of strong feelings has subsided. Note what you are thinking while experiencing the wave of emotions, but only talk about that after the wave has passed. Boiled down, the rule becomes, 'be quiet, feel the feelings, then talk about the experience.'"

(2) Helper, say, "Here are some other guidelines to communicate to you. It is that we will respect your pace. This is not a race. This is a delicate process of personal discovery. Like a school bus stopping for railroad crossings, we stop if you need time to process, even to 'catch your breath,' so to speak. If you need to take a longer break in order to move on, that will be fine too. I am here to be of assistance to you. This is your recovery journey to be experienced at the pace that fits best for you."

(3) Helper, continue, "I would like you to remind yourself of the truths addressed in these affirmations. Repeat them after me: 'I did not cause the acts of abuse. (pause) I was an innocent child deserving protection. (pause) I was hurt, but I am not broken. (pause) What was done to me or in my presence was wrong, but I am on my way to being free of the impact.' (pause) It is recommended that you write these truths down and place them in a prominent place in your home. Make a commitment to review them daily."

(4) If your S is concerned that he or she does not recall many details of the events, remind him or her that, "It could be a signal you used dissociation to cope with the traumatic experience. I assure you that if you were present and alive, the details are recorded in your memory. The program will help your recall of details that will become more robust. This process

is like putting together a 500-piece puzzle. You begin with the corner pieces, then you work on the edges as you move in towards the center. Eventually, all the pieces fit perfectly together. The same is true with each new discovery; more details will emerge. As you uncover more of your truths, more of your life will start making sense. This experience is part of the recovery journey. The details will come forth as you work and process the steps."

(5) If your S believes he or she cannot do the steps, this could be a remnant of the shame that some S's experience. Their beliefs seem to indicate that because they were abused, there must be something inherently wrong with them. They think they must be broken. This has been labeled as a "shame-based identity." This too will begin to fade away as the S becomes aware they are not damaged goods. They were just fine before the abuse happened. They will experience their "wholesomeness" and their capabilities beginning to return. Your S will start to feel alive again, free to love and be loved. They will begin to feel capable, to have and achieve goals, to make mistakes, and be able to forgive. (Helper, relay the thoughts from this paragraph in your own words and in your own way to your S.)

b. Helper, give your S a copy of the sheet with the 9 categories of abuse listed. It can be found in Appendix B, "Outreach Response Survey." Ask him or her, "Look through this list and mark if any of these things happened to you." (This could be given as a homework assignment to do before the next session.) If your S marked any, ask your S, "Talk about what comes to mind when you think about that category? What feelings, if any, are stirred up? Use the I-message format. 'When I think of_____, I feel_____.'"

c. Helper, prepare your S for going more into the descriptions of the abusive categories. Direct him/her to Appendix C, "Expanded Description of Types of Abuse." This Appendix goes into greater detail about each of the 9 categories of abuse. Ask your S, "Read the material and make brief notes on the worksheets with blank spaces for each category of abuse that apply to you." Ask your S, "Bring these back to the next session."

2. Getting more into the details of one's abusive history.

a. Review the worksheets your S made from reading the expanded descriptions of the 9 categories of abuse in Appendix C.

(1) Ask the S, "Take time if you are ready to read aloud the notes you wrote on the worksheets as you read the material in the expanded descriptions of the categories of abuse." As before, take time for your S to feel any waves of emotion before talking about them.

(2) Then, say to your S, "Using the I-message format, describe the experience of making the notes now as you begin reporting about them."

(3) Encourage your S to keep the worksheets handy because he/she may need to add more details about the already noted events. Even more memories might be revealed from the next exercise of discovery.

b. Getting all the memories and recording known details.

(1) Helper, if your S did not complete the worksheets or if more memories have come to mind, ask, "If any more details of what happened have come to mind, record them as best as you can." Once your S has recorded any additional notes, go on.

(2) Helper, say, "To discover if there are any more details about memories, I will be asking you in a moment to shut your eyes and go inside to discover if there are any more events to recall." The instructions about how to do this follow. Say to your S, "Before we proceed, do you have any questions?" Helper, answer any questions and when you sense this is complete, go on.

(3) Helper, say, "As mentioned before, close your eyes and go inside. Ask yourself if there are any more memories to note? S, be patient and be ready to note what comes to mind. Take all the time you need, there is no hurry." Keep asking softly, "are there any more memories to recall? We want them all."

(4) Helper, give your S time to note anything that might come up. While your S is checking what may be coming up, say in a soft, slow voice, "Take your time to note any new information that might be coming up. If you sense you are getting something, raise a finger to let me know you are getting another memory. If you are getting more than one or even several, raise your finger a couple times to indicate you are getting more. That is great if you are."

(5) Helper, if your S is getting more memories, continue to tell him or her, "Take time to note what you are remembering. Review any details of the scenes to let me know in a moment what you

are getting. Just note what is coming to you now. We will talk about the new details once you are done. Take your time. Let me know when you have finished."

(6) Once you get the signal that your S has finished, say, "That's just great. Close the scene in your mind's eye. Open your eyes and let's hear what you saw."

(7) Helper, listen. If it all seems right on track, ask him or her, "Now start recording what you viewed onto the worksheets as related to the category of abuse being recalled."

c. A time to reflect on what your S is experiencing with this sharing of more details about the abuse.

(1) Once that information has been recorded (the blank lines filled in), ask the S "What are you discovering and what is being revealed to you from this process?" Helper, listen. It is okay to express your empathy for what you are hearing. As appropriate, say things like, "That was awful, but you are doing a great job of recovering the details."

Here are some other examples of things to say:

"No child should have to have faced that abuse."

"Remember, you were a child deserving to be protected."

"You did not do anything to cause that abusive behavior."

(2) Then, ask your S, "Use the I-message format to describe this experience of recording and talking

about more of the details. ('When I think of _____, I feel_____.')"

3. **Beginning steps of putting the abusive history together.**

   a. Beginning to fill in the Master List of Abusive Events (MLAE) found in Appendix E.

      (1) Helper, bring out the MLAE. Take as many sheets from the packet as needed with one for each event or episode.

      (2) Explain how this will work for the S by saying, "Each page will reflect an abusive event. The event number and a brief description will be detailed at the top of each page. For example, Event # 1, Episode at Mike's cabin. He sexually abused me."

   b. Fill in the Master List of Abusive Events with what is known.

      (1) Ask the S, "If you are ready, start transferring the information from the worksheets as appropriate onto the MLAE for each episode. Fill in all that is known so far. Leave items 7 to 17 blank because this information most likely will not be discovered yet. The answers to these activities will be revealed from the activities of Chapter 4."

      (2) Ask the S to "Look at the Master Sheet (s) and reflect on what it is like to look at it or these even though they are not complete yet."

   c. Start putting the story together.

      (1) As the S looks at the information gathered to date, ask him or her, "Begin writing out your story about

what happened for each event remembered. You can write these on the back of the sheet." Helper, give your S plenty of time to write out his or her story.

CLOSING REMARKS

Helper, say to your S. "You have been incredibly brave as you have begun uncovering, recording and speaking about what happened to you. Let me remind you that you are not broken, that you did nothing to cause this abuse to happen. You are well on your way to getting free of the hurtful impact of this abuse. You were a child. We will continue on in the next chapter digging deeper for the details of the abuse and the impact. I know that you will continue being brave and courageous in the next stages of your recovery journey."

CLOSE FOR THE HELPER

Helper, take a moment to close your eyes. Bring into your mind's eye the reality you and your S have now achieved by standing on the second large rock preparing to step onto the third large rock. The water is rushing all around but you both remain dry. You make note of the next rock to safely step onto as part of moving across this stream making progress to eventually reach the far bank. For a moment, also take note of the surroundings, the fresh air, the breezes moving through the trees, the comfortable temperature and the soothing sound of the rushing water.

Simultaneously, you become aware the topic of this chapter has been a heavy one. There is no getting around the notion that offenders acting out onto innocent children is abhorrent and disgusting. You did not judge your S. You know your S did the best he or she could do to survive. You do not judge him or her. Your S did not cause the abusive acts. With each step he or she takes, the hope is ever increasing that full recovery is attainable. There is no question that you will continue to support him or her as a patient, caring guide.

Now, it is time to move further into the part of the journey that asks the S to face more of the hurtful facts including the impact that occurred in the abusive events. Helper, your skill level truly will call you to reach higher. I know you will rise to meet the challenge. Before moving on, take a slow deep breath in, hold it and then slowly exhale completely. Breathe in again slowly, hold it for a moment and then slowly exhale.

Imagine beginning to step across to place your foot onto the third large rock. As you are securely in place, reach out for your S's hand and gently guide him/her onto this third steppingstone. When you are safely standing on this third rock, open your eyes as you let the image fade away and be gone.

When you are ready, step into the next chapter, Chapter Four.

Chapter Four
Searching for the Painful Details Brings New Freedom

INTRODUCTION

In this chapter, Helper, you will be shown how to help the S use visualization to reveal significant information from the painful memories. It will be used to discover if there are any more events to be listed onto additional *Master List of Abusive Events* sheets. Then, the S will begin the life-giving review of the hurtful scenes. If needed, remind your S as appropriate that this review of the hurtful events is not as painful as it was in the original experience. Helper, hang on. Your skill level is about to experience one of the most powerful, creative expansions while assisting your S in understanding the role the early hurts have played in his or her life.

1. **Laying the groundwork for reviewing the details of the early, painful scenes.**

   a. **Review the details that have been placed on the Master List of Abusive Events sheet or sheets.**

   (1) Helper, ask your S, "Look at the MLAE sheets that have been created to date. Review the details that have been entered." As your S completes this review, say "Ask yourself if any additional details have come to mind either about the events already noted or maybe even new scenes have come to mind. Take time to record this new information before we go on."

(2) If he or she has discovered more, allow your S time to fill in the new details. Say to your S, "Be aware that you might discover that you want to make additions and/or corrections to what has been recorded so far. This is a typical part of the process of putting your painful history together. You might re-write the details of scenes several times as new information comes into your awareness."

b. **Say to your S, "As you do this review, be thinking about in what order you would like to do a more detailed review of the scenes."**

(1) Say to your S, "In whatever sequence you would like, place the MLAE sheets in the order in which you would like to review them." The S is to think about the order in which he or she would like to review the early scenes and place them in that order. Typically, it would be in the order in which they happened, or your S might have reasons to do it differently.

2. **How to discover if there are any more memories or scenes to put on a Master List of Abusive Events sheet.**

a. **Setting the stage for using visualizations to check if there are more events to note.**

(1) Helper, say to your S, "This will be the second time to invite you to go inside with eyes closed to discover if there are any more events of which to be aware. The beauty of going inside is to learn about how one's subconscious works. The creativity available is incredibly awesome."

(2) This brings to mind one of the stories from the treatment center of how an S would go into a

nearby woods as a child after experiencing a traumatic event. She would imagine flower fairies coming out of the blooms to talk to her. The flower fairies provided great, needed comfort. The experience to her at the time was a message of hope that things were going to be okay. She was loved and all she had to do was to keep hanging in there.

(3) Helper, explain, "In a moment you will be asked to close your eyes and be invited to ask the subconscious some questions. Pay attention to what comes to mind once the questions have been asked. The point is that we will be looking for other events that need to be remembered, if there are any. We want them all. Then again there may not be more."

b. **The S will begin the journey into learning to interact with his or her subconscious.**

(1) If the S is ready, ask him or her, "Close your eyes and go inside. Find your mind's eye. Bring your attention to what comes to mind after you ask the following question of yourself. The question is this, (Helper, say this in a slow and soft voice) 'Do I have any more memories of hurtful events that happened to me and need to be noted?'"

(2) Then offer this to your S: "You are only to notice if you get any new remembrances. Do any new ones come to mind in your mind's eye? Take all the time you need and just notice what you get."

(3) Helper, be patient as you repeat in a soft, slow voice, "Take all the time you need to note if you are getting any new remembrances. Give me a signal when you sense you are done."

(4) Helper, when your S indicates he or she is finished, say, "Open your eyes and reveal any newly discovered memories. If there is no new material, that is fine. If some new revelations came up, let's talk about them."

c. **If any new material was noted, record it on the *Master List of Abusive Events*.**

(1) Say to your S. "Record any new details of events already recovered. If you discovered a new event or maybe several, record the answers on a new sheet or sheets. Use as many as needed. Record items of what happened such as the type of abuse, who was the offender(s), where it happened, your age, and what time of year it was." Say to your S, "Once any new information has been recorded, state in what order you would like to view the abusive events scene by scene. Let us number the MLAE sheets in the order you want."

3. **Getting to the details and the impact of the early hurtful events.**

a. **This section will focus on the review of the abusive events and the reporting of the answers to the remaining questions listed on the MLAEs.**

At the end of this sequence, all of the details about the events will be completed. An incredible amount of self-awareness will occur about how the S's life had been influenced by the early learnings. The method of making physical contact during the review with a touch of the wrist will be introduced. Helper, this skill sequence is absolutely powerful as you literally watch the personal insights come forth from the S.

b. **A review of the steps getting to the details of what happened and what the impacts have been.**

(1) Helper, explain to the S what is getting ready to happen. Say, "In a moment I will ask you to close your eyes as before and ask you to go inside. I will ask you to begin bringing up the hurtful events in the order we have agreed to review them. Your job is to note what happens from the beginning, through the middle of the sequence of events, until you get to the end. Then we will work together to record the information on the MLAE for each event."

(2) Tell your S, "As we get started, I will ask you to find the beginning scene where the hurtful event #___ started and ask you to place it in your 'mind's eye' on 'pause'. While on 'pause' note where you are in the scene, who is around, what do you hear, what time of year is it, how old are you, what time of day it is, what is the temperature and what is the weather like. I will apply a light touch on your wrist as you begin to 'run the scenes.'"

(3) "Once you are oriented to what is happening in the opening scene of event #__, I will ask that you let the scenes of this event unfold from the start until the end. Your task is to note the details of each scene including what happened to you, your thoughts and your feelings. If a strong wave of feelings comes over you, stop, note what you are experiencing and feeling. When ready, and the wave has passed, proceed on."

(4) "Every event has a beginning, middle and an ending. When you have finished, open your eyes. I will release the light touch. When you are ready, we will record the answers to the remaining

questions listed on the *Master List of Abusive Events."*

(5) "Once the recording of your answers is complete, we will move on to reviewing the remaining hurtful events, one event at a time. Depending on how long this takes, it may take several sessions to complete the review of all the scenes. If you are okay with this, as you are watching your scenes, I will apply a light touch on your wrist. I will apply this from the beginning scene until you have completed your review. Then, I will release it. If you have any questions, this is a good time to ask them."

(6) Once the questions have been answered, ask your S, "Are you ready to begin the review or continue the review of Event #_____?" When you get the signal to start, present the following to your S.

c. It's time to review a hurtful scene.

(1) Helper, say, "Close your eyes. As you go inside, ask yourself to bring up the first scene of the event we agreed to start with (or continue with the review of other events that have already started). Begin reviewing the scene. In a moment, I will activate a soft touch on your wrist as a way to remind you I am here with you all the way. Be aware while you are doing your review; this will not be as upsetting as experiencing the original scene was. When you are ready, bring the beginning scene into your 'mind's eye.' This is the place in which the event begins to unfold. Place it on 'pause.' Look around in your mind's eye and pay attention to what was happening in this first scene. Where are you? Who is around? What

noises do you hear? Note where you are, what you are doing, and what time of day and year it is. Let me know what you are noticing as you keep your eyes closed and focused on this scene."

(2) Helper, listen to your S's report concerning the details of this beginning scene. Say to your S, "When you are ready to proceed, let me know."

(3) When you get the signal to proceed, say in a soft and gentle voice, "Let the scene begin to unfold." (Helper, establish a gentle touch on the wrist and continue to speak in a soft and gentle manner as you deliver the instructions to your S.) "Take all the time you need as you watch the beginning, move into the middle of the sequence, and head to where it ends. All events have a beginning, a middle, and an end. Your job is to learn all you can about what you are experiencing, feeling, and thinking. "

(4) "Keep moving through the scenes until you reach the end. If something needs to be reviewed, you can back up and watch it again. You can review the parts as many times as you would like until you get what you need to know. This is your recovery journey. "

(5) "Should you experience a strong wave of emotions, move your visual screen away, making it small until the wave passes. As suggested earlier, note what you are experiencing while the wave comes and then fades away. This is your recovery, no one else's. Let me know when you have reached the end."

(6) When you receive the ending signal, ask your S, "Open your eyes as I release your soft touch (we will refer to this as an anchor)" and ask, "What was that like?" Helper release the anchor.

(7) Once your S is finished recounting what that was like, move on to answering the questions from the Master List.

(8) Recording the details onto the Master List of Abusive Events.

    a. Complete the remainder of the unanswered items on the Master List for this event just reviewed. This is completed when all items have been answered and recorded.

    b. Then, keep repeating the review of each hurtful event on the list until they have all been reviewed and the data recorded on the Master List. This means returning to paragraph c. (1) on page 42 and repeating the steps.

    c. Note: If this review needs to be scheduled in multiple sessions, do so as convenient.

(9) Reflect on the details of the Lists for this and all events that have been reviewed and the answers recorded.

    a. Ask your S, "Look over the items recorded for each event and then let us talk about what this experience is like." If you need to continue at another time, then set that time. The point is to take time to reflect on the data recorded for each event. Then, do the same for each event until they have all been reviewed and the data noted as recorded.

b. Ask your S, to "Reflect on the experience from completing the review of all the hurtful events."

CLOSING REMARKS

When all the painful events have been reviewed, say this, "An absolutely great and powerful job. My hat is off to you for the incredible bravery you displayed reviewing all those scenes and identifying your truth about what happened as you noted the impact and the costs to your life. This is the beginning of what recovery is all about. You are standing on your truth, your thoughts and feelings. These are not up for debate."

Speaking for the author to the S and Helper, "You and your guide both deserve to congratulate yourselves. The S is experiencing what it is like to move into a good recovery by facing the reality of each hurtful event and identifying the impact. Well worth every moment just to be in this place. More experiences are on their way for which you will be forever grateful."

CLOSE FOR THE HELPER

Helper, you were a great assistant in this process. While reviewing the details and recording them, you have been aware that your S is changing. His or her life is beginning to make more sense. Your S could not have completed this without your stable hand. Wow, what a ride this has been! There are more great experiences yet to come. Keep hanging on to being curious and trusting the process.

It is time to close your eyes as you return to the scene in the woods in which you are standing on the third large steppingstone along with your S. Be aware of the sound of water rushing around you. Notice the next steppingstone is a stretch but within reach. You are approaching the middle now. The far bank is getting closer but still it remains a ways off yet. You become aware there is no turning back now. Imagine preparing to stretch your leg towards this fourth large stone. It appears to be large enough to accommodate both of you. To make it, you must remain focused as you move to shift your balance placing both feet onto the new stone. As before, you turn towards the other person and reach out to them to bring that person onto the fourth rock safely with you. As you complete that move, you sense your confidence growing that you will be safe in reaching the far bank if you keep being patient, trusting your ability to move carefully as you keep your faith. Open your eyes as you let the scene fade away knowing you can return to it later.

When you and your S are ready proceed on to Chapter Five.

Chapter Five
Bringing the Precious Child and the Hurt Younger Selves Together

Under the Protective Care of the Adult Self: What a Wonderful Reunion

"Those who help you in life are like pillars on the porch. Sometimes they hold you up, and sometimes you lean on them. Sometimes they may lean on you. Most importantly, it is just enough to know they are nearby."

—Unknown

INTRODUCTION

a. Helper, your skills keep growing by leaps and bounds. I realize that with this chapter you are past the halfway point in this journey of leading your S into knowing his or her true self as the fake facades begin to fade away. There are more incredible skills ahead for you to learn. When you have completed your part of the journey, you are going to be ready to lead other S's into a great, solid recovery. All the S has to do is follow your lead. This is truly a monumental achievement for you wherever you choose to take it.

b. This part of the journey to recovery addresses that which was most blatantly absent from the hurtful scenes – the protective presence of a loving caretaker. Helper, this is where your ability to be patient and trusting of the process is vital. At this point, you will encourage the S to go inside to discover his or her Precious Child (PC). It is a time for this reality of the Precious Child to soak deeply into your S's awareness. This discovery opens the door to a wave of fresh hope. It goes something like this: "If I were whole once, then maybe I can be whole again."

c.   This part of oneself is the S before the impact of the abuse has occurred. What follows typically in the S's development after the abusive events is the development of some version of a pretend or false self. This is about surviving. With the revelation that this precious self exists, the S will be open to the reality that a normal, successful, and fulfilling life will now be more possible. Helper, almost before your very eyes, you will experience the S beginning to cast off the shackles of the impact of the hurtful memories and begin to view him or herself and the world in a more positive and hopeful way.

1.   **Taking time to absorb the realities recorded on the Master List of Abusive Events.**

   a.   S is to take time to study the Master List of Abusive Events.

      (1) Helper, ask your S, "Take time to continue to study the reality of what the details mean that are recorded in the Master List of Abusive Events. Be aware of the ages you were at the time of the event(s), the kind of abuse, the offender(s), and anything else that catches your attention. Be especially cognizant of the cost to your life. What is this information telling you?"

   b.   S is asked to be aware of the losses and what the S has been carrying all these years.

(1) Ask your S, "Be especially aware of the costs to your life. Include in this awareness what was lost. In addition, be very clear about what you have been carrying all these years that you are ready to let go of and not carry any longer."

(2) Ask, "S, speak about this experience of looking at the information recorded on the *Master List of Abusive Events*. Include what you lost and what you have been carrying but want to release."

(3) Helper, encourage your S by saying, "Speak about this awareness. Use the I-message format: When I think of _____ , I feel_____ ."

2. **Seeking the creativity of the subconscious, again.**

   a. Going inside to discover the S's Precious Child.

   (1) Helper, in a soft voice say to your S, "Close your eyes. Go inside as before and invite your creative self along with all necessary internal skills to find your Precious Child. This is that part of you before you were abused. Bring him or her out so you can see and experience him or her."

   (2) Helper, be quiet and patient as the process unfolds in its own timing. As you might feel the need to be of support, say softly, "Take all the time you need. Your creative abilities will find and bring this Precious Child out for you to see and experience. This event is like no other. There is no hurry. It cannot be rushed. Creativity does not work that way.

   (3) As you remain patient, remind yourself that you have memories of others smiling and speaking to this younger self. You may have seen that self in the mirror. You might even have seen pictures of this self. He or she is there. Just be patient and

trust the process. Let me know when you see this precious one in your mind's eye."

(4) Helper, when you get the signal that S has found his or her Precious Child, feel free to join with the joy of the moment. Maybe even become part of a small celebration which might spontaneously break out. Words of support you might offer would be: "This is wonderful. Enjoy the moment, for this has been a long time coming."

(5) Helper, say to your S, "Take all the time you need to get to know this child. Notice how really precious he or she is. He or she is free to be his or herself. He or she is free to love, be loved, and forgive. He or she is also free to explore and be curious to make mistakes. Note that he or she treasures each moment and is excited about life." (Let your S know it's okay to hug this part. Helper, you might offer a pillow or stuffed animal for S to hug as he or she does this in imagination too.) Then say, "Lastly, let me remind you that your Precious Child is a part of you and your life."

(6) Ask your S, "Open your eyes and describe what this experience is like."

(7) Once this has been shared, continue on.

3. **Precious Child and all the hurt parts are to meet.**

    a. While the S is enjoying getting acquainted with the Precious Child, say, "Close your eyes and go inside again. This time it is to invite all parts of yourself that were hurt to come out to meet your Precious Child. Let me know when all parts have come forth."

b. Helper, as before, be patient while the hurt parts come out. Once you sense that they are all in your S's mind's eye, invite your S to offer this information to all these parts. "S repeat after me: This is our Precious Child, which is a part of us before the abuse started. I want you to become well acquainted with one another. (Helper, pause as appropriate.) As the healing continues, you who have been hurt will get to take on some of the Precious Child's qualities. Eventually you will embrace them all. These qualities include being free to live and knowing who you are. Be assured that you have a wonderful future awaiting you and can now give love as well as receive love. You can make mistakes and be curious. Best of all, you will be able to forgive. You each will become a part of one another. These abilities will continue to develop as you grow, mature, and change."

c. Give your S plenty of time to watch these hurt parts of himself or herself become better acquainted. Say to your S, "Let them play and get to know one another. Give me a signal when this seems complete."

4. **Preparing for your S to parent this group.**

a. Helper, with his or her eyes closed, invite your S to talk to this group as follows: "One thing that was missing from these hurtful and traumatic scenes was the protection of a caregiver. It would have been helpful if you were just held and comforted after an abusive event. Having someone available to say, 'It is going to be okay' would have been healing."

(1) Ask your S, "Open your eyes when you are ready and describe what you are experiencing at this moment." Once the comments are finished, go on.

b. S, in his or her own words, accepts the role of parenting this group.

(1) Say to your S, "Close your eyes again and go inside. In your own words tell these wonderful parts of you that you are taking over the parenting. Imagine gathering them around you. Let them know that you survived. Invite them to look at you, their adult self."

(2) Once this is complete, go on.

c. Let them know that you are committed to protecting them.

(1) As before, say to your S, "In your own words, let them know you are committed to protecting them. The offender(s) will not hurt them again. In the next piece of work, you are going to confront the offender/offenders on their behalf and settle some issues that are long overdue."

(2) Once this is communicated, have your S open his or her eyes and comment on this experience.

CLOSE FOR THE HELPER

a. The fact that you are safe to be with is evidenced in this part of the work. You were trusted to share in the experience of your S discovering his or her Precious Child. What a precious, intimate moment! Great job. You have got the heart for this work.

b. Helper, you have been doing a great job listening and absorbing new skills. Most important has been letting your S know you are compassionate about his or her getting free of the impact of the abuse perpetrated onto him or her. I commend you. With every step accomplished, you are helping this world be a better place. The extension of this is that as you integrate these skillsets into your repertoire, you will be a lifeline for unrecovered S's who need what you know.

c. Helper, you are more than halfway through guiding your S through this healing journey. The first time through, it is understandable that it takes a great deal of concentration. It will get easier each time you work through it. By assisting another S become free of the impact of an abusive event, you are providing a wonderful service to all the world.

d. This is an excellent time to return to your adventure in the woods, as you close your eyes and be aware of standing on the fifth rock among this fast-moving water. You note the progress you have made as you are beginning to be halfway across and are making your way across the fast-moving waters. You really are about to move past the halfway point now. That far bank is some distance away yet, but definitely getting closer. The rocks remaining look to be large enough, spaced just right and quite stable to allow for you to finish. But there are still five more to go anyway you look at it. With patience and concentration, you will be across before you know it.

e. Be aware of the next rock to move onto. Stretch out your leg and move your weight to balance onto the next rock. As you feel stable, look back to your partner, imagine reaching out your hand as you pull him/her toward you. Once the other person is securely on this next rock, be aware how your confidence has been growing in your ability to skillfully navigate as you move from rock to rock with the rushing water racing around you. Now it is time to let this scene fade away.

Open your eyes and when you are ready, continue on to Chapter Six.

Chapter Six
S Confronts Offender(s), Then Forgives

INTRODUCTION

a. In this chapter, you will be introduced to the steps which will lead the S through the process of using imagination to confront his or her offender or offenders with the truth about what happened and the impact from being abused as a child. This will be about the S getting his/her recovered identity and power back. Helper, be prepared for this process of supporting your S standing up to the offender or offenders by studying all the material in this Chapter from start to finish. Presenting the details of the abusive events to the offender or offenders will seem totally real to the S. It will be an additional demonstration of how powerful the use of imagination can be.

b. The S is encouraged to express feelings as intensely as the S is able on the "exchange part" (this is when the S gives up what has been carried but is ready to let go of, along with taking back what was lost). Assist your S with completing items 14 and 15 on the MLAEs that your S has filled out so far. This is the last exercise before the process of forgiving one's offender or offenders is completed. Helper, ensure that your S is very detailed and specific about what is being exchanged when it is time for that process. In addition, ensure your S is being honest and sincere with the heartfelt expression of feelings. There is to be no holding back here. If your S seems to be holding back, I encourage you to assist him/her in the full and robust expression of the feelings.

You might say something like, "You have good reason to be absolutely furious about what your offender did to you. Let your offender feel the full intensity of your anger and pain." Helper, your part is to encourage and maybe even demonstrate how to effectively confront, but only model or encourage enough for the S to pick up the idea and then being able to continue on his/her own. The point is to not do it for the S but to assist him/her in standing up effectively for himself/herself as if they are totally involved and committed in delivering the confrontation.

c. Expression of strong feelings can have its complications as has been addressed previously. The offender or offenders may have threatened to hurt the S more if he/she ever told anyone. Sometimes more pain would be inflicted on the S for any expression of strong feelings during the abusive event or events. The S may display some hesitation because of his/her own history of exploding with emotions at times that have caused difficulties. If your S is displaying some of this kind of hesitation, I encourage you to be an advocate in this situation. Be exceptionally clear that it is okay at this time in the healing process to express his/her truth accompanied by any strong emotions that come up. Helper, trust your own intuition here and do what feels right for your S.

d. If you are like me, I had no specific method for how to lead someone into forgiving an offender. This material will answer the question of how you lead a person to the point where he or she can truly forgive an offender or multiple offenders. Helper, you will be learning how to do exactly this. One of the key concepts to facilitate this process is by inviting your S to make clear the distinction between the person and the behavior. Abusive acts are never forgiven. They remain forever wrong. But we can forgive the imperfect human being. As before, this will be accomplished through visualization methods.

e. Unforgiveness left unchecked tends to lead to other unwanted outcomes like venting unresolved anger when the situation does not call for it. Harboring unresolved anger can bring on depression or set the stage for the S to do offensive things. This can include the venting of anger towards others who may not be offenders or even display offensive behaviors. The possibility also exists that one could unload with both barrels on some other person who does display offender tendencies. Because being free of unforgiveness can be a good thing for one's physical and mental health, helping your S be free can truly be life-giving. This aspect of the benefits makes this process of forgiveness essential to complete.

f. The primary focus of this chapter is to allow the S to experience standing up to his or her offender(s) with the total unabridged truth about what happened and what the impact has been. This could be described as the S getting his/her power back by overcoming the shame-based identity and in the process find his/her own identity.

g. Then, once your S learns to separate the person from the behavior, forgiveness will make more sense than it did before. Once the S can embrace the wisdom of forgiving the person, not the behavior, it becomes more understandable, and therefore more achievable for the S to complete successfully.

h. The final activity is for the S to experience forgiving him/herself. Peace flows in where any unforgiveness was.

A. Preparing to Confront the Offender(s).

1. Ask your S to review the details recorded on the MLAEs.

(a) Helper, say to your S, "Take time now to again review the details recorded on the Master List(s) from Appendix E (helper do the same). The purpose of this is for both of us to become extremely familiar with all the details. If I need to assist you in recalling any information as you confront your offender or offenders, I will. Sometimes in the middle of the intensity of the confrontation, it is not unusual to lose track of some of the details. This could be especially helpful during the 'exchange' portion of this process (#14 and #15 of MLAEs). Be aware in this review of what the offender(s) did to you, what age(s) you were, what the impact has been, how your thinking changed, what you lost and want back, what you want to give back that does not belong inside you, note what you took forward into your future and what your feelings were. Be really clear about what happened to you and the cost to your life. You were an innocent child who deserved to be protected!"

(b) Once your S indicates that he or she has finished the review, go on.

B. Choosing one of the 3 pathways to proceed forward

1. **Say to your S, "What follows are descriptions of three pathways for moving forward depending on the number of offenders that abused you.** The first option, (2a), is chosen when you have one offender to confront. The second one, (2b), is selected when you are dealing with more than one offender but choose to confront one at a time. The third path, (2c), is chosen when you had several offenders, and prefer to deal with them as a group, all together at one time. Let's discuss the options and agree which path fits the best." Once the best path is selected, proceed to 2a, 2b, or 2c.

2a. This choice is when there is one offender.

(1) Say to your S, "This option is chosen when you had one offender, and you want to deal with him/her. If this is your choice, we will continue on unless you have some questions." Once you think your S agrees with this path and you think your S understands this option, then continue on.

(2) Say to your S, "We are going to prepare you for dealing with your offender by himself/herself. Close your eyes and go inside. Activate the screen in your mind's eye. Imagine that we have asked your offender to come for a meeting with you. Can you also imagine that he/she has just arrived in the parking lot and is in the process of getting out of his/her car as he/she heads for this building?" If your S can imagine these developments, proceed on.

(3) Continue by saying, "If you are ready, first imagine inviting all your hurt parts and your PC to come out from their respective timelines to be near or playing nearby while we confront your offender. Know that what we are about to do should have happened at the time of the abusive acts. We love you all and want you to experience being protected while your offender is being confronted. While we hold the offender to task, you are to stay just close enough to experience what it is like to be protected and safe. How are your PC and hurt parts doing?"

(4) Listen to your S and if your S is ready, say, "Imagine your offender coming into the building and waiting in the hallway down from this room. How does your offender look so far?" Listen to your S and if he/she seems okay, explain, "In a moment, I will invite him/her into our room. What is his/her name?" Helper, listen to the name and make sure you heard accurately say, "Am I understanding correctly that you are ready to invite _____ (Offender's name) into this room?"

(5) "If that makes sense and you are ready, I will invite him/her to come on in. As he/she comes in, I will direct him/her to sit in the chair we have set up. I will explain the basic rules. These are for the Offender to remain quiet while you present your truths, and he/she is to remain seated until you are finished." Once you have the signal from the S, continue on.

(6) Helper direct your voice down the hallway, as you say, "_____ (Offender's name), come on

in." (pause, as the Offender enters,) "Be seated." (Helper, motion towards the chair). Helper, now say "(S's) name) _____has some things to say to you about how you hurt him/her and some details about how that hurt has impacted him/her. You are to remain quiet and stay seated until he/she has finished and releases you to go. Is that clear?" Once the Offender gives an affirmative, go on.

(7) Say to your S, "This is your time to explain in detail what happened to you. Include in the details the impact and responsibility you are placing squarely in his/her lap. This is not a time to apologize or be polite or politically correct. This is a time to be brutally honest. As you begin, make sure the chair is placed the correct distance from you where it feels comfortable." If the chair is placed where it works best, go on. "As you begin telling your truth, rely on your responses as recorded on your MLAEs. I will assist you if you need me. I have full faith in your ability to stand up for yourself effectively and assertively."

(8) Helper, have the appropriate MLAEs handy for you to reference. Your primary task is to support your S being totally honest, brave, specific, even assertive and maybe aggressive as appropriate with the confrontation. This is to be done while presenting the painful details of the abusive events. Even though the details have already been reviewed and recorded, your S may get stuck recalling some of the details as things will undoubtably become intense. The issue could be that the S is experiencing strong waves of

emotion and may just need encouragement that expressing the anger, the rage, the extreme hurt is totally understandable. He/she has a right to vent it all. Here is where your own judgement comes into play. If your S is having difficulty recalling details, you can assist. If your S is shooting and hitting his/her offender with both barrels, so to speak, then just keep being an encourager.

(9). If your S becomes hesitant and somewhat reluctant to stand up for his/her truth, you might demonstrate how the confrontation can go with conviction and appropriate assertiveness. Remind him/her that this is a time to let this offender have it.

(10) To a reluctant S say, "This is the right time and place to speak with a strong voice as you stand up for your truth to your offender. Remember the costs to your life. Remember the terrible feelings and what you did with them. Remember how your thoughts changed about your family, yourself and your future. Remember what you wanted and did not get. You have a right to be absolutely furious at this offender." Helper, you may even need to model for the S how to speak up for him/herself. Check the answers as recorded on the MLAEs and ensure that your S has addressed them all. Save processing and assisting with #14 and #15 to the end before your S is asked to forgive this offender.

(11). If your S remains reluctant to be assertive, take a moment to ask, "Might there be some internal resources that could help you become more comfortable with being assertive in this task? It might be a symbol of comfort or courage. It might be the image of a close friend, a coach or mentor, maybe even a religious figure like Jesus. Go inside and find that creative resource you need to get the energy and resourcefulness to confront your offender." If your S locates some creative resource that helps him/her proceed with confidence, then go on.

(12). If your S's offender has any trouble obeying the rules say, "We can introduce methods to keep the offender behaving while you confront him/her. This could include using duct tape to go over his/her mouth or to tape his/her arms to the chair in a way to assure he/she remains seated in the chair."

(13). If your S has effectively addressed the details of the abuse, the impact, the costs and ready to work through #14 and #15, explain to your S, "This step calls on your internal creativity to help. First, I ask that you recall what you lost that you want returned. What do you want back?" Give time for your S to get in touch with that which was lost that he/she wants to get back. Once your S has clearly identified what was lost, ask, "Now go inside and find a way to creatively make something that can stand for and represent that what was lost and you want returned. Once you have created this representation, let me know." Once your S identifies this symbol, proceed on.

(14). Say to your S, "Tell your offender what you lost that you want returned. Tell them what you are taking back now that belongs to you." Once that is completed, proceed on.

(15). Tell your S to say to the offender, "This image represents what I am taking back that you took from me. As you say this, imagine that you are taking back what was lost, say 'I am taking back what you took from me. I am now receiving it back in my space, my spirit.' Imagine this is back into your body." Once that is effectively in place, ask your S, "What is it like to have that returned to you? Describe your experience." When that is completed, go on.

(16). "Now I will lead you through identifying what you have been carrying, that you want to give up (#15 of MLAEs). Take a moment to create in your imagination a representation of that which you have been carrying that does not belong any longer. Let me know when you have named and created this representation. Open your eyes and say what you are giving back." Once this is completed, go on.

(17). "Now, close your eyes again and imagine this creation leaving your body, your spirit, and returning to your offender. Say to your offender, 'Here is _____. This does not belong with me any longer. I am giving this back to you.' Imagine this that you created leaving you and returning to your offender." Once that transfer is complete, say to your S. "Describe what this experience has been like?" Once your S has described this experience, proceed on.

(18). This last step involves forgiving your offender.

(a) Helper, ask your S, "Look at the offender and from the center or core of your being, tell the offender this: I have made a conscious decision today to forgive you totally and completely for the abuses you perpetrated onto me. (Pause between sentences as your S repeats them.) I do not condone any of the ways you hurt me. (Pause) These acts remain forever wrong. (Pause) For my sake, I am releasing any and all unforgiveness I have been harboring toward you. (Pause) Any anger, hatred, resentment, or disgust I had been feeling, I am letting these go only to evaporate into the atmosphere. (Pause) I speak peace and freedom over myself and all the parts of me you abused. I claim today in this moment that I am totally free." Take a moment to let this experience soak in. Helper, when you sense your S is done with this, go on.

(b) Helper, ask your S, "Before we tell him or her to go, check inside yourself. As you think about this offender, are you carrying any remaining tensions as a sign there may still be some unforgiveness to deal with?" Give your S time to do this. If things are clear, then go on. If not finished, go to the next note below.

Note: If there are some unresolved issues yet, say to your S, "Go inside and use all creative resources necessary to discover what is left undone. Find a way to let it go. When you are done, let me know." When your S is finished, go on.

(c) Helper, tell your S to release his or her offender by saying, "You can go now. Watch him/her leave until the image is gone." Ask your S, "Comment on what this experience was like?" When your S is finished, go on.

(19). Helper, ask, "Think of your Precious Child and the other younger selves brought out to experience being protected. How are they doing?" Listen. When his/her observations of these parts are complete, go on.

(20). Helper, say, "It is time to return all these parts we invited out to return to their respective timelines. We thank you all for your involvement today. You all get to keep the peace that comes from being protected and the peace that goes along with forgiving others. Take time to hug them and express your love for each one. Let me know when they are all back in their places." When that is completed, continue on.

(21). Before ending this part of the session, ask your S, "Give a report on how this experience of standing up to your offender has been for you. What is going on inside right now? Include in your comments how the hurt parts and PC have been impacted by this experience of being protected and also what did they think of this process?" When your S has finished sharing his/her thoughts, feelings and impressions, then go on to 3. Forgiving One's Self (on page 92).

2b. Say to your S, "This option is chosen when you had several offenders, and you want to deal with them one at a time."

"If this is your choice, we will continue on. If you have any questions, now is the time to bring them up." Once you think your S agrees with this path and understands this option, then continue on.

(1) Say to your S, "We are going to prepare you for dealing with your offenders one at a time. Close your eyes and go inside. Activate the screen in your mind's eye. Imagine that we have asked your offenders to come for a meeting with you. Can you also imagine that they have just arrived in the parking lot and are in the process of getting out of their cars?" If your S can imagine these developments, proceed on.

(2) Continue by saying, "If you are ready, first imagine inviting all your hurt parts and your PC to come out from their respective timelines to be near or playing nearby while we confront your offenders. Know that what we are about to do needed to happen at the time of the abusive acts. We love you all and want you to experience being protected while your offenders are being confronted. While we deal with the offenders, you are to stay just close enough to experience what it is like to be protected."

(3) Listen to your S and if your S is ready, say, "Imagine your offenders coming into the building and waiting in the reception area past the hallway down from this room. How do your offenders look so far?" Listen to your S and if he/she seems okay,

explain, "For a moment, decide who you would like to invite in first?" Listen for the name. Affirm that you heard correctly by saying, "I understand that you want (Offender #1's name) _____ to come in first. Right?" Listen for your S to affirm that you heard correctly. Explain, "We will confirm the name of each offender you want to confront as we send one on his/her way and prepare to bring the next one from the reception area."

(4) Say to your S, "When we invite each individual offender in, I will direct him/her to sit in the chair you have set for him/her. I will call your offender by name. as we call him/her into this room. He/she is to not talk but to be quiet and just listen to you. The offender is to remain in the chair until released by you." If this is clear for your S, continue on.

(5) Helper, direct your voice towards the reception area as you call the first offender's name. "_____ (Offender's name), you can come in now." (Motion toward the chair.) Sit there. As _____ (S's name) talks about the ways you hurt him/her. You are to remain quiet and stay in your seat. He/she will detail the impact the abusive events have had on his/her life. When he/she is finished, you will be released to go."

(6) Once the rules are clear, say to your S, "Take a moment to look at what you see, think and feel as you look at him/her sitting in the chair. Also, is the chair placed in comfortable distance from you?" Listen to your S and answer any questions or

address any issues. If everything seems okay, ask, "Are you ready to proceed?"

(7) If your S is ready to proceed, say, "You can begin telling him or her your truth. You can present all the details of what he/she did to hurt you and how this impacted your life. Present this in great detail relying on your responses as recorded on your MLAEs. I will assist you if you need me. I have full faith in your ability to stand up for yourself."

(8) Helper, have the appropriate MLAEs handy for you to reference. Your primary task is to support getting your S into being totally honest, brave, even assertive and maybe aggressive as appropriate with the confrontation while presenting the details of the abusive events. Even though the details have already been reviewed and recorded, your S may get stuck recalling some of the details as things will undoubtably become intense. Here is where your own judgement comes into play. If your S is having difficulty recalling details, you can assist. If your S is shooting and hitting his/her offender with both barrels, so to speak, then just keep being an encourager.

(9) If your S becomes hesitant and somewhat reluctant to stand up for his/her truth, you might demonstrate how the confrontation could go with firmness, conviction and appropriate assertiveness. Remind him/her that this is a time to let this offender have it.

(10). To a reluctant S say, "This is the right time and place to speak with a strong voice as you stand up for your truth to your offender. Remember the costs to your life. Remember the feelings and what you did with them. Remember how your thoughts changed about your family, yourself and your future. Remember what you wanted and did not get. You have a right to be absolutely furious at this offender." Helper, you may even need to model for the S how to speak up for him/herself. Check the answers on the MLAEs and ensure that your S has addressed them all. Save processing and assisting with #14 and #15 to the end before your S is asked to forgive this offender.

(11). If your S remains reluctant to be assertive, take a moment to ask, "Might there be some internal resources that could help you become more comfortable with this task? It might be a symbol of comfort or courage. It might be the image of a close friend, maybe a mentor or even a religious figure like Jesus. Go inside and find that creative resource you need to get the energy and resourcefulness to confront your offender." If your S locates some creative resource that help him/her proceed with confidence, then go on.

(12). If your S's offender has any trouble obeying the rules say, "We can introduce methods to keep the offender behaving while you confront him/her. This could include using duct tape to go over his/her mouth and/or to tape his/her arms in a way to assure he/she remains seated in the chair."

(13). If your S has effectively addressed the details of the abuse, the impact, the costs and ready to work through #14 and #15, explain to your S, "This step calls on your internal creativity to help. First, I ask that you recall what you lost that you want returned. What do you want back?" Give time for your S to get in touch with that which was lost that he/she wants to get back. Once your S has clearly identified what was lost, ask, "Now go inside and find a way to creatively make something that can stand for and represent that what was lost, and you want returned. Once you have created this representation, let me know." Once your S identifies this symbol, proceed on.

(14). Say to your S, "Tell your offender what you lost that you want returned. Tell what you are taking back now that belongs to you." Once that is completed, proceed on.

(15). Direct your S to say to the offender, "This image represents what I am taking back that you took from me. As you say this, imagine that you are taking back what was lost as you imagine that item leaving your offender and coming back into your body, your spirit. Once that is effectively in place, note what that is like to have that returned to you. Describe your experience." When that is completed, go on.

(16). "Now, I will lead you through identifying what you have been carrying, that you want to give up (#15 of MLAEs). Take a moment to identify and name what you have been carrying that you want to give back." Helper, listen to what your S wants to give up then go on. "S, now create in your imagination that which you have been carrying that does not belong. Let me know when you have created this representation. Open your eyes and say what you are giving back." Once this is completed, go on.

(17). "Now, close your eyes and imagine this creation leaving your body, your spirit, and returning to your offender. Say to your offender, 'Here is _____. This does not belong with me any longer. I am giving this back to you.' Imagine this that you created leaving you and returning to your offender." Once that transfer is complete, say to your S, "Describe what this experience has been like?" Once your S has described this experience, proceed on.

(18). Say to your S, "This last step involves forgiving your offender."

(a). Helper, ask your S, "Look at the offender and from the center or core of your being, tell the offender this: 'I have made a conscious decision today to forgive you totally and completely for the abuses you perpetrated onto me. (Pause between sentences as your S repeats them.) I do not condone any of the ways you hurt me. These acts remain forever wrong. For my sake, I am releasing any and all unforgiveness I have been harboring toward you. Any anger, hatred, resentment, or disgust I had been feeling, I am letting these go only to evaporate into the atmosphere. I speak peace and freedom over myself and all the parts of me you abused. I claim today in this moment that I am totally free.'" Take a moment to let this experience soak in. Helper, when you sense your Survivor is done with this, go on.

(a) Helper, ask your S, "Before we tell him or her to go, check inside yourself. As you think about this offender, are you carrying any remaining tensions as a sign there may still be some unforgiveness to deal with?" Give your S time to do this. If things are clear, then go on. If not finished, go to the note below.

Note: If there are some unresolved issues yet, say to your S, "Go inside yourself and use all creative resources necessary to discover what is left undone. Find a way to let it go. When you are done, let me know." When your Survivor is finished, go on.

(19). Helper, tell your S to release his or her offender by saying, "You can go now. Watch him/her leave until the image is gone." Ask your S, "Comment on what this experience was like?" When your S is finished, go on.

(20). Helper, ask, "Think of your Precious Child and the other younger selves brought out to experience being protected. How are they doing?" Listen. When his/her observations of these parts are complete, go on.

(21) If there are more offenders waiting to be confronted, continue on.

(22). Say to your S, "How do your offenders waiting in the reception area look so far?" Listen to your S and if he/she seems okay, explain, "For a moment, decide who you would like to invite in next?" Listen for the name. Affirm that you heard correctly by saying, "I understand that you want (next offender) _____ to come in next. Right?" Listen for your S to affirm that you heard correctly.

(23). "As before when we invite each next offender in, I will direct him/her to sit in the chair you have set for him/her. I will call your offender by name. as we call him/her into this room. He/she is not to talk but to be quiet and just listen to you. The offender is to remain silent while you explain what happened to you, as you reveal what he/she did to you."

(24)."Are you ready to invite your next offender into this room?" If your S is ready, ask "What is the name of the next one to be called." Once your S gives you the name of the next offender say to the offender, "(Offender's name) _____, you can come in now." (Pause) "Be seated." Once the offender is seated, say, "You are to listen and not say anything while _____ (S's name) is talking. He/She has some details to present to you about his/her truth of how you hurt him/her and how you impacted his/her life. You are to remain seated until you have been released to go." Once the offender seems to understand the rules, say to your S, "Take a moment to look at what you see, think and feel as you look at him/her sitting in the chair? Also, is the chair placed in the right distance from you?" Listen to your S and answer any questions or address any issues. If everything seems okay, ask, "Are you ready to proceed?"

(25). If your S is ready to proceed, say, "You can begin telling him or her your truth. You can present all the details of what he/she did to hurt you. Present this in great detail relying on your responses as we recorded on your MLAEs."

(26). Helper, have the appropriate MLAEs handy for you to reference. Your primary task is to support getting your S into being totally honest, brave, even assertive and maybe even aggressive as appropriate with the confrontation while presenting the details of the abusive events. Even though the details have already been reviewed and recorded, your S may get stuck recalling some of the details. Here is where your own judgement comes into play. If your S is having difficulty recalling details, you can assist. If your S is letting his/her offender get hit with both barrels on his or her own, so to speak, then just keep being an encourager.

(27). If your S becomes hesitant and somewhat reluctant to stand up for his/her truth, you might demonstrate how the confrontation could proceed with conviction and appropriate assertiveness. Remind him/her that this is a time to let this offender have it.

(28). To a reluctant S say, "This is the right time and place for you to speak with a strong voice as you stand up for your truth to your offender. Remember the costs to your life. Remember the feelings and what you did with them. Remember how your thoughts changed about your family, yourself, your future, what you wanted and did not get. You have a right to be absolutely furious at this offender." Helper, you may even need to model for the S how to speak up for him/herself. Check the answers on the MLAEs and ensure that your S has addressed them all. Save assisting with #14 and #15 until the end.

(29). If your S remains reluctant to be assertive, take a moment to ask, "Might there be some internal resources that could help you become more comfortable with this task? It might be a symbol of comfort or courage. It might be the image of a close friend, a coach or mentor and maybe even a religious figure like Jesus. Go inside and find that creative resource you need to get the energy and resourcefulness to confront your offender." If your S locates that resource or resources, then go on.

(30). If your S's offender has any trouble obeying the rules say, "We can introduce methods to keep the offender behaving while you confront him/her. This could include using duct tape to go over his/her mouth and/or to tape his/her arms in a way to assure he/she remains seated in the chair."

(31). If your S has effectively addressed the details of the abuse, the impact, the costs and is ready to work through #14 and #15, explain to your S, "This step, as you will recall from before, calls on your internal creativity to help. First, I ask as you look at the offender that you recall what you lost that you want returned. What do you want back? Once you find it, tell me what that is." Give time for your S to get in touch with what was lost that he/she wants back. Listen to what has been lost. Then go on.

(32). Once your S has clearly identified what was lost, ask, "Now go inside and find a way to creatively make something that can stand for and represent that what was lost, and you want returned. Once you have created this representation, let me know." Once your S identifies this symbol, proceed on.

(33). Say to your S, "Tell your offender what you lost that you want returned. Tell him/her what you are taking back now that belongs to you." Once that is completed, proceed on.

(34). To your S say, "Imagine that you are taking back now what was lost as you imagine that item leaving your offender and coming back into your body, your spirit. Once that is effectively in place, note what it is like to have that returned to you. As before, describe your experience." When that is completed, go on.

(35). "Now I will lead you through identifying what you have been carrying, that you want to give up (#15 of MLAEs). Take a moment to identify that which you want to give up. Name what that is." Helper, listen to what the S is giving up. If your S has been specific enough, go on.

(36). Say to your S, "Now, close your eyes and imagine creating something that can represent that which you want to give up, that does not belong in you. Let me know when you have this representation created." When your S indicates he/she has the new creation, go on.

(37). Tell your S, "Close your eyes and in your imagination see this creation leaving your body, your spirit, and returning to your offender. Say to your offender, 'Here is _____. This does not belong with me any longer. I am giving this back to you.' Imagine this that you created leaving you and returning to your offender. Once that transfer is complete, describe what this experience has been like." When he/she has described this experience, proceed on.

(38). This last step involves forgiving your offender.

(a). Helper, say to your S, "Look at the offender and from the center or core of your being, tell the offender this: 'I have made a conscious decision today to forgive you totally and completely for the abuses you perpetrated onto me. (Pause between sentences as your S repeats them.) I do not condone any of the ways you hurt me. These acts remain forever wrong. For my sake, I am releasing any and all unforgiveness I have been harboring toward you. Any anger, hatred, resentment, or disgust I had been feeling, I am letting these go to allow them to evaporate into the atmosphere. I speak peace and freedom over myself and all the parts of me you abused. I claim today in this moment that I am totally free.'" Take a moment to let this experience soak-in. Helper, when you sense your Survivor is done with this, go on.

(b) Helper, ask your S, "Before we tell him or her to go, check inside. As you think about this one, are you carrying any remaining tensions as a sign there may still be some unforgiveness to deal with?" Give your S time to do this. If things are clear, then go on. If not finished, go to the note below.

Note: If there are some unresolved issues yet, say to your S, "Go inside and use all creative resources necessary to discover what is left undone. Find a way to let it go. When you are done, let me know." When your Survivor is finished, go on.

(c) Helper, tell your S to release his or her offender by saying, "You can go now." Watch him/her leave until the image is gone. Ask your S, "Comment on what this experience was like?" When your S is finished, go on.

(39). Helper, ask, "Think of your Precious Child and the other younger selves brought out to experience being protected. How are they doing?" Listen. When his/her observations of these parts are complete, go on.

(40) If there are more offenders waiting to be confronted, return to (21) through (40) until the last offender has been confronted and forgiven.

(41) When all the offenders have been confronted and forgiven, say, "Thank you PC, the hurt parts and any supportive images that were brought in to assist, can be released to return to where you came from. Thank you for your help."

(42) Ask the S, "What has this been like?" Helper, once your S is finished, include your own

experiences too. When this is completed, continue onto 3. Forgiving Oneself.

2c. This pathway describes the option for bringing in multiple offenders at the same time.

(1) . Helper, as is true throughout this chapter, your assistance is key. I am asking you to read through all the steps of 2c. to get an idea of the sequence for assisting your S in dealing with this group of offenders.

(2). Helper, say to your S, "You have several decisions to make."

(a). "One is to take a moment and review this choice, If you remain pleased with your choice of bringing them in all at once, say you agree." If your S agrees go on.

(b). "The next choice is to decide the setting you want to pick for the group in which to gather. It could be that you prefer for them to come into an auditorium, a gym or a theatre. Typically, there are a lot of similar issues across various abusive events, so you can address many offenders simultaneously. Name your preference for where the meeting is to take place, and we will proceed."

(c) "The next choice concerns whether you prefer for them all to be standing in a line side by side or theatre style. Let me know your choice."

(d) "The final choice concerns how you want to address them. It could be to have them step forward from a line, stand by their seat, or to sit in a chair or chairs like in a 'hot seat' or 'hot seats.' When you are finished with that one or a group, he/she/they can step back in line or sit down or return to their seats. As before, let me know your choice." Then go on.

(3) Helper, ask your S, "Close your eyes. Go inside and activate the screen in your mind's eye. Can you imagine that all of your offenders have arrived in the parking lot? Can you see them getting out of their cars and following the signs directing them as to where they are to gather in a waiting area?" Watch for your S's response and if he/she can imagine this scene, then move on.

(4). Here is an outline of the sequence of steps in this process. Say to your S, "I will speak to the group about them remaining quiet and then turn the program over to you. Once you have confronted the group about how they hurt you and you have laid out the details of the impact, I will invite you to conduct the 'exchange.' This involves identifying what was lost that is to be returned. Likewise, you will define what has been carried that is to be given back to the offenders. We will complete this before speaking forgiveness over your group of offenders. This will be accomplished by using your creative power like a painter making a brush stroke over the entire group. Do whatever seems right for you to do."

(5) Say to your S, "While the group is gathering in the waiting area, it is time to invite your PC and all the parts of you that were hurt to come from their places in their timelines and join you. Tell them where you would like them to be while you confront the offenders that hurt them. This is the

part that was missing in the original scenes. You were not protected, and the offenders were not confronted. Today, we will be confronting these offenders with the truth. We assure you that these offenders will not hurt you again. They are to remain silent and not move unless directed. Let me know when you are through placing these precious ones where you want them while we do this work. Let me know when you have finished. Open your eyes. Tell me what it was like having them close to you." Listen, and when your S is done. proceed on.

(6). Tell your S, "Think for a moment. Do you have a preference as to how you would like them to come in from the waiting area? Is there some rationale for some being first or last and who might make up the middle half of the group? You might not have any preference as to an order. If you do have a preference, identify that preference. If it does not matter in what order they enter, that's fine too. This is your recovery work, so whatever you select is just fine. Once you have indicated your choice, let me know and then we will proceed on." Listen for the preferences and proceed on to honor your S's choices.

(7). Say to your S, "Close your eyes and access the window in your mind's eye. Can you see your offenders in the waiting area?" If 'yes,' then ask, "How are they doing?" Listen to your S, then ask, "Are you ready to stand up for yourself to these offenders?" If 'Yes,' then go on. If S has a concern, listen and find a way to resolve it before proceeding on.

(8) Helper say to the group assembled, "Let me have your attention. Please proceed quietly to the large meeting area." (Gym, theatre, large auditorium). (Helper is to direct the group to stand or sit as S had requested.) To your S say "Can you imagine your offenders filing into the place you have arranged for them to gather? See them coming in one by one into the larger auditorium, gymnasium, theater, or whatever area you selected. As they go by, advise them by saying, "Remain quiet and prepare to listen to your S's truth." In a firm voice, instruct them to remain standing or be seated, whichever you prefer. They are to remain standing or seated until you are ready to deal with each one, a small group of offenders or the group as a whole. Let me know when they are all seated or standing and behaving. Also, let me know if there are any problems."

(9). Tell your S, "It is time to present your truths to these offenders about what happened. Your truths are not up for debate."

(10) The script for confronting the offenders is basically to present the information from the Master Lists. This is to be applied to each offender or groups of offenders in the manner decided above. This includes the entire group. The next task for the S is to complete the "exchange" before forgiving them all.

(11) Helper, address S and ask, "How does this look to you? How are you feeling about this?" Listen to your S's response.

  i. *Note* to the Helper: If your S seems reluctant, use your judgment in adding protections or words of comfort as needed. If your S is experiencing any anxiety, hesitation or fear about doing this work, this is especially important. I want you to remember this is very real to your S. Consider this might be a time to remember to use the relaxation methods in Appendix G.

ii. Note. If you have to stop and put protection in place, do so. You can suggest some options as listed above such as placing armed guards next to them, duct taping their mouth, or putting chains and tape around their bodies to keep them in their chairs. S could bring in supportive comforts such as a blanket, a pastor, or relative who could be a source of comfort and encouragement. This source of comfort could be Jesus Himself. Let your S choose. Say to your S, "Let me know when you are ready to go on."

iii. Note: Helper, be aware that on one previous occasion the S dealt with the offenders en masse. Meaning, the S had them standing in a line beside one another. Then, as they stood together, he or she told each one what he or she had done to hurt him or her. Then, the S went over what the abuses and impacts were. The S told each one something such as, "And the same for you, you, and you." Then, when done, the S forgave them en masse also.

(12) Say to your S, "If you are ready, imagine dealing with this group of offenders in the way you have selected. Call each one into the chair on the stage or have each one step forward where S is. You may have selected to leave them where they are

while you focus on each one by looking at him/her. Whichever way you selected to proceed, begin doing that. You can do it out loud or quietly inside. Do take note of your feelings and be sure to express the feelings that arise."

Note: to Helper: Deliver the prompts as necessary from the MLAEs. Speak in a slow, soft voice with plenty of time in between your prompts to give your S time to come up with the next items. Helper, say, "Begin with how old you were, where the events happened, what time of year and day it was, and most significant, what was done to you. Explain what your feelings were and what you did with your feelings. Describe how the events that occurred changed your perceptions of yourself, your family, your authority figures, and your future. Name what you lost and are taking back now. Be clear and specific about what you have been carrying that you are now giving back. Identify what you took into your future as a consequence of the abusive episodes."

(13) Helper, keep repeating these items from the Master List as needed. Say them softly and slowly until you sense your S is getting finished or doing just fine with the process on his or her own. As appropriate, it is okay to strongly encourage intense expressions of emotions and thoughts when referring to elements in the episodes as well as about those things that your S is taking back and giving up.

(14) Say to your S, "This is a time to be exceptionally honest and thorough. We are not worried about being politically correct. We just want raw honesty accompanying true feelings. If you are

having any difficulty, let me know. When you sense that you are done, let me know that too." When you get the indication that your S is done, go on.

(15) Helper, say to your S, "You will be done when you have told them all that was on the Master List and you cannot think of another thing you need to do or say."

    i. Note: To the Helper: Vary your instructions based on the methods your S chose. Feel free to assist with recalling the items on the Master List as a way of prompting your S's memory as needed.

(16) This segment will be to complete the "exchange." This means identifying what was lost and the S wants back as well as identifying what he/she has been carrying that he/she is now going to give back.

(17) Ask your S, "Identify what was lost as a result of the abuse, that you now want back. Name the losses and when this is complete, we will go on."

(18) Say to your S, "Take time to create images that will represent those things that you lost. Then address the group by saying: 'I am now taking back from each of you what I had lost.' S, imagine all that you lost returning into your body, returning back into your spirit. Tell me what that is like and then we will continue with the exchange."

(19) Now, begin to identify those things you have been carrying that you are ready to give back. Helper, say to your S, "Identify those things you have been carrying from this group that no longer belongs in you. Look around, identify those things

you are giving back. Use your creativity to make an image of the things you are returning. Imagine these things leaving your body and spirit. Seeing them entering the offenders body and spirit. By your focused look you will indicate who you are returning these to.

(20) Helper, say to your S, "Now it is time to forgive your offenders."

(a) "Look at each offender and from the center or core of his or her being, tell each one this: 'I have made a conscious decision today to forgive you all totally and completely for the abuses you perpetrated onto me. I do not condone any of the ways you hurt me. These acts remain forever wrong. For my sake, I am releasing any and all unforgiveness I have been harboring toward you. Any anger, hatred, resentment, or disgust I had been feeling, I am letting these go only to evaporate into the atmosphere. I speak peace and freedom over myself and all the parts of me you abused. I claim today in this moment that I am totally free.'" Helper, when you sense your S is done with this, go on.

(b) Helper, ask your S, "Before we release the offenders, check inside yourself. As you think about each one, are you carrying any tensions as a sign there may still be some unforgiveness to deal with?" Give your S time to do this. If things are clear, then go on. If not finished, go to the note that follows.

Note: If there are some unresolved issues still, say to your S, "Go inside and use all creative resources necessary to discover what is left undone. Find a way to let it go. When you are done, let me know." When your S is finished, go on.

(21) Helper, tell your S to release all his or her offenders by saying, "You can all go now." When you get an indication, they are gone, go on.

(22) Helper, ask, "Think about your Precious Child and the other younger selves brought out to experience being protected. How are they doing?" Listen. When his or her observation of these parts is complete, go on.

(23) Helper, say, "It is time to return all these parts we invited out to return to their respective timelines. We thank you all for your involvement today. You all get to keep the peace that comes from being protected and the peace that goes along with forgiving others. Take time to hug them and express your love for each. Let me know when they are all back in their places." When this is completed, go on.

(24) Helper, say, "Now it's time to release any and all support people and/or things. They are to go back from where they came. When that is all complete, let me know." When that is complete, go on to Section 3, Forgiving Yourself.

(25) Ask your S, "What was that like? How do you feel now?" Listen. When your S is done, you can express your experience as a Helper assisting in this part of the work. Take time to express your appreciation for the hard work your Survivor put into this. When this is complete, go on.

3. **Forgiving Yourself. Close your eyes and visualize yourself.**

(a) Helper, tell your S, "Before we end this session, there is one more important task to take care of. With your eyes closed again, I want you to put yourself out in your mind's eye. Let me know when you can see yourself, the 'you' that is right here today. Let the image of you float into your mind's eye. Turn that image of yourself so you are looking at one another." Helper, give this a few moments to occur. When you get an indication that this has occurred, go on.

(b). Helper, tell your S, "This 'you' has all your timeline memories from the time of the first abuse and the impact until now. Access this awareness. Let me know when you are ready to go on." When you get a signal that your S is ready, go on.

(c) Create a collage of your memories in need of forgiveness.

(1) Helper, say, "As you look at yourself, be aware of those parts of you that have done things of which you may not have been proud, knowing that a lot of painful, extreme things may have been your way of dealing with or coping with the old trauma. Nonetheless, in your mind's eye, take time to see you in those scenes that you know you were acting in or acting out something from your painful past. These may include you acting out of your value system.

(2) Once you can see these scenes, put them above you like constellations in the sky. Arrange them like you are creating a collage. No matter how many there might be. We want them all out in your mind's eye. When you can see them, let me

know." When you get a signal, your S can see all these scenes, go on.

(3) Helper, ask your S, "Tell me, what is it like to look at these?" Once your S is finished telling you his or her experience from looking at these scenes, go on.

(d) Forgiving yourself:

(1) Helper, say, "If you are ready, I am going to lead you through the process of speaking forgiveness over yourself. Those times you acted out of your value system, maybe you offended someone, or maybe you offended yourself or hurt someone. Maybe you lied or at least misrepresented the truth. It does not matter what you did. What does matter is that you thoroughly, completely without hesitation, are willing to forgive yourself without question. If you are ready to go on, let me know." When you get the signal that your S is ready, go on.

(2) Helper, say, "Repeat this after me: 'I release all of those parts of me from unforgiveness, guilt, shame, and any resentment I may have been harboring about myself and my history. I forgive you totally and completely without question.' Let me know when you are finished and all the items you put on your collage are now forgiven and gone." Give your S some time to experience and process this. When you sense that your S is done, go on.

(3) Helper, give a moment for this experience to soak in, so to speak. Then say, "If you are done with that, now tell yourself, 'You are part of me, and I invite you back inside. We get to keep the forgiveness, and I commit to 'us' that I will learn

how to take these learnings into the future, and along with that learning about how to have highs and lows. I commit to learning how to live in moderation at least most of the time. I also will learn to deal with present time reality as just that. I will keep improving on checking out how much of what I am about to do might be about my old past and how much it is about my present. I commit to living in the present, drawing on the new past of how things could have been and should have been.' You two now become one as you let this forgiven self to come back into you. Now, let that forgiven you and those new parts you brought out from your past go back inside where they belong in your timeline." Give some time for your S to process this last instruction. When ready, go on.

(4) Ask your S, "Open your eyes and comment on what you experienced during this part of the process of forgiving yourself." When this is completed, Helper, go on.

Close for the Helper

a. What an awesome piece of work this segment has been! Helper, you were absolutely magnificent and have matured so much. If a bit of celebration seems appropriate at this juncture, I would agree. Let your S know how proud you are of the progress he/she has made. You two do what seems right for the occasion right now in the moment. There is no question, Helper, you have cleared a major hurdle. Awesome, awesome job. There are no words to appropriately express the power of what you helped your S do. Nothing but life changing.

b. At this point, as we stand back to look at the big picture, it becomes so clear that you and your S have come a long way together. Helper, you deserve a great deal of credit for your patient role in this journey. I am also sure that you have noted more changes coming over your S as he or she absorbs the lessons in each chapter. We began with being clear about feelings as different from thoughts as we moved into reviewing and recording the details of the abusive events. Then came the powerful work in confronting and then assisting your S in forgiving the offender(s). Then came your S forgiving himself or herself. Wow! There is no question you have helped your S come a long way in this journey toward recovery.

c. Let's re-visit the imagery of your progress in crossing the stream. Close your eyes and bring the scene into your mind's eye. You are definitely past the halfway point now. The bank is getting closer and closer. You still have to be careful, for the water is still fairly deep between here and the bank. You need to stay focused with full concentration.

d. As before, prepare to transfer your weight onto the next rock. Once you are firmly standing on this next one, reach out for your partner's hand. As you notice that he/she is standing next to you, take a moment to note how far you two have come. That once far away bank is getting closer. Allow yourself to briefly celebrate your accomplishment as you are aware that you have remained dry as you have moved from stone to stone. While it will require the same careful concentration to navigate across the remaining rocks, you note you are filled with a confidence that tells you, you can actually reach that once far bank successfully. With that, take a moment to note the sound of the rushing water, the light breeze moving through the trees, the warmth of the sunshine and the happy sounds of the birds fliting from limb to limb. Now is the time to let that image begin to fade away. Open your eyes, knowing you can return to this scene later.

e. When ready, proceed on to Chapter Seven.

Chapter Seven
Re-Writing Your S's Abusive History

"Imagination is more important than knowledge."

—Albert Einstein

INTRODUCTION

Helper, hang on. Because you are about to help your S tap into a long-awaited discovery of the truth of how your S wished the abusive event(s) had gone. Of the over 300 trauma survivors I have worked with, it never fails when the S is asked about the way an S wished the hurtful events had gone, the answer literally just flows into their mind's eye. It is almost like magic. But what a powerful resource as you will be assisting your S in creating a new history using the dynamic abilities that are available in one's imagination. Let's get on with this dynamic process.

1. **Preparations for creating a new history.**

    a. Helper, the first task is for you to take time to read through the steps in this chapter for re-writing a scene from your S's abusive past.

        (1) Study these steps thoroughly. The skills presented in this segment of the journey of recovery are the most sophisticated yet.

        (2). Study the details recorded on the Master List of Abusive Events sheets. Get the big picture of the

97

abuse and the impact that has remained from these harmful events.

(3). Say to your S, "This is a good time to decide on the order in which to review the hurtful events. Let me know what you prefer." When it is clear what he or she has decided, then go on.

2. **Re-writing the hurtful scene(s)**

   a. **Bring out the Precious Child and all the parts hurt by the abusive events.**

   (1) Say to your S, "Close your eyes as before. Go inside and invite your Precious Child and the parts that were hurt to come out into your mind's eye." As you get a signal that is complete, continue on.

   (2) Then have your S explain to these parts what is coming next. Have your S say, "As you know, I am from you. I am a part of your future. You and I did survive. Today, you are going to get to experience a new version of the abusive events. You will get to keep this new version to take with you when you return back into your respective timelines. We will later learn how to get to take these new learnings about how it should have been into our future."

   (3) Ask your S, "How are these parts of you liking this possibility?" Listen to your S's response and then go on.

   (4) Helper, invite your S to address the hurt parts. Ask your S to say, "As we work on rewriting the hurtful scene(s), I will ask the one who experienced the impact of the episode we will be reviewing, to be right here beside me. So, I will ask that part to stay close until we are finished. I

believe each of you will like the new changes." When this seems completed and your S is ready, go on.

b. Twenty-five steps to rewriting your abusive history.

(1) Step 1: Helper, say to your S, "It is time now to let each part of you that was abused rewrite his or her story. To begin, using your creative resources, decide where you want your Precious Child and that part or all of those parts to be while we work with each one to rewrite his or her history. It is a matter of having them be where it feels right for you. We will invite each one to come by you as we focus on his or her memory, and then we will invite him or her to experience the new version. Let me know when you have them all where you want them to be. You are the parent of these parts. You could have them right beside you or close by or not right at your side. You could even have them go play together while you call each one up to do the rewriting of his or her scene. Let me know when you have them all where you want them."

Note: If there was only one past hurt, then suggest that one stay right there with your S. Adjust the instructions above and below to be consistent with dealing with one part.

(2) Step 2: Helper, once you get the signal that everything is in place, tell your S, "I will review the steps that are coming. Like when we watched the episode originally, I am going to touch your wrist on the place we used before as you review the event. This time after the review is done, I will release the anchor or touch and ask you to go back

to the beginning scene again. I will ask you to hold it like on pause in your mind's eye.

(3) Step 3: "In this step, I will use a second finger to touch a spot next to the first one as you begin to create the new version of the scene. When you have finished, I will release this second anchor and ask if you liked the new version. Then, I will ask you to go back and place the beginning scene on hold. If you need to re-do this new version, then I will re-set the second anchor as you create this newer version. Again, I will ask for you to return to the beginning scene and place it on pause. If you are happy with the new version, I will activate the anchors as you run both scenes, the original one and the new one on top of one another. You will be given instructions to let the new one become blended into the first one until the old one is gone. Only the new one will remain. I will hold both anchors until the blending is complete. Later, I will be releasing them when you let me know when only the new scene remains. Let me know when you understand what is coming and you are ready to go on."

(4) Step 4: Helper, when you have the signal to go on, say, "Now invite that part of yourself that was first (or next on the list if you are continuing to work on other events) on the list to come beside you. Let me know when he or she is there." Once you get the signal that part is in place, go on to (5).

(5) Step 5: Helper, say to that part, "We are so deeply sorry that you had to suffer those hurtful memories. We do thank you for being willing to show us that hurtful episode again. You will not have to relive this anymore. In a moment, after we

review the original hurtful scene, we are going to let you watch and experience a new version of the memory. This is done with the aid of our creative resources, and this new version will be the way you knew it should have happened. It will be the one you knew you wanted and deserved."

(6) Step 6: "You will get to keep this new one. You will be able to know the other one happened, but the new version will be for you to use when you think of the past. Bring that first scene, the one where this began (or the next one if you are working on several) back into your mind's eye. Put it on pause like before. Let me know when you two are ready to proceed." When you get the signal, they are ready, go on to Step 7.

(7) Step 7: Helper, gently say, "Like before, hold that first (or the next) scene for just a moment until it is time to go on." (Helper, establish the first physical or kinesthetic anchor: the touch on the wrist.) Helper, when you have the anchor in place and your S is ready to proceed, say, "Go ahead and watch that episode again. Once that is done, go back and put that original beginning scene back in your mind's eye and hold it on pause like before. Let me know when you have reviewed the old one and have the original first scene (or the next in the sequence) back again on pause." Helper, release this first anchor.

(8) Step 8: When you get the signal that the review is completed, give your S time to comment on what that review was like. Helper, ask, "Do you have any comments on what that was like this time?" Proceed on when he or she has finished with the comments.

(9) Step 9: Once you have the signal to go on, Helper, prepare to set a second anchor and tell that young part, "We thank you again for watching that hurtful episode. We regret that you had to suffer at all. You did not deserve that abuse. You were a child. You deserved to be protected. When that painful episode happened, you knew then exactly what you wanted and needed."

"Now, we ask that all the necessary internal creative resources be available so you can create the episode to be just the way you wanted it to happen. Let me know when you are ready to go on."

(10)   Step 10. When you get the signal, say, "Now, with your eyes closed, go inside to access any and all creative resources to be available for the version you deserved to have happen." Helper, set the second anchor as your S begins to watch the new creation. Hold it until it is completed. Softly remind him or her, "Take all the time you need. This is your story now, the way you deserved for that scene to have happened. Let the new episode unfold, just the way you wanted it to be. Note your feelings, what you do, what you say, and what you think in this new version. You can go back and renew any part you would like. When you signal you are finished, this will be the one you get to keep." Helper, as you talk about the first or the second anchor, press that one a little harder for emphasis. We will refer to that as a 'bounce.'"

(11)   Step 11: Helper, say, "Let the new scene (bounce second anchor) become the version you wish you could have had instead of the one you received back then. In the new one" (bounce the

second anchor) you can see yourself being loved, protected, and comforted. See the version you know you wanted (bounce second anchor). "See the new scene unfold just the way you wanted it to be."

(12)   Step 12: Once you get the signal from your S that the new version is complete, ask, "How did that new version look?" Wait for your S's answer, then proceed, saying, "How is this younger self liking this new version?"

(13)   Step 13: Wait for this answer. Then say, "At this time I will re-set the first anchor as I also hold the second anchor. (Bounce each one for emphasis.) Go back to the beginning and place the original scene along with the new one, so both will be on pause. Next, run the new version simultaneously with the original scene and let the new one become blended into the first one in such a way that the first one disappears. Take a moment to let the new one become blended into the first one. Only the memory of the new one will remain. Let me know when that is completed." When you get the signal that the blending is complete, release the second anchor and say to your S, "This first anchor now represents the new memory. We will refer to this anchor as the 'New History' Anchor. The memory of the old one is gone now. Release the first anchor. What do you think of this new memory you created?" Listen. When the sharing is completed, go on.

(14)   Step 14: Continue, saying, "For a moment, (Reset the new history anchor) can you imagine how life would have been different if the new version had happened? Take a moment and let the

new version unfold and play into that younger self's future. See how life would have been different back then. Let me know when you have reviewed that reality."

(15)   Step 15: Wait for your S to experience this and invite any comments he or she wants to offer. Once his or her comments are done, ask, "Would you like to keep this new change in such a way that the younger part of yourself gets to use this one along with the extensions of the benefits of this new version? When you have thought about that, let me know what you are experiencing."

(16)   Step 16: Listen to your Survivor's response. Then say, "Let me know when you are ready to move on." When you get the signal that your S has explored that difference this change would have made, go on.

(17)   Step 17: Say, "Take time for that part of you to become immersed in the reality of the new version. Let that part become familiar with how life would have been different. Take time for that part to soak up the reality of how life would have unfolded with the new version. To help that happen, we are going to ask that, as before, you use all the creative resources inside to let this become a part of your new history. It is yours to keep. Let me know when you can see the full extent of how differently life would have been."

(18)   Step 18: Once you get the signal that the blending is complete, ask, "How does that younger self like this change and how does this look to you?" Listen and then say, "To that younger self whose memory got rewritten, say,

'You get to keep that as you return to your place in your timeline. When you think about that time of your life, you can know the other happened. But you can now also remember this new one along with how life could have been if the new one had happened. You can now act as if the new one did happen. In a moment, we will be letting all of those parts of you that were abused do the same thing, so you all will have new memories to take into your future. How does that younger self like that?'" Wait for your S's report and then go on.

(19) Step 19: Say to your S, "To the part that just re-wrote the scene, you get to take this new version of the memory inside along with the qualities of the Precious Child that you did not get to have or had been lost."

(20) Step 20: Tell your S, "Using all necessary creative resources inside, bring him or her in, updated for the age of this younger self. As you experience that, I will be making a 'zipping' sound to resemble closing a Ziploc bag."

(21) Step 21: Helper, make the sound of a slow, extended zip by saying, "zzzzzzzzzzzzzzip." Tell your S, "Give me a signal when that is completed."

(22) Step 22: Once that is completed, say, "You (younger self) can try on these qualities and use them right now. You are free to be, to feel, to think, to love, to have fun, to be curious, to make mistakes, and to forgive. _____ (Survivor's name), watch this younger self using these qualities again. Tell me what you see." Helper, give your S time to tell you his or her observations and feelings. Be aware that this

process of taking on the qualities of the Precious Child in that younger self may have occurred spontaneously already with the enacting of the new memory and its extension into his or her future from the time of the hurtful event.

(23)   Step 23: Helper, to your S say, "Go ahead and ask this younger self to return to his or her place in your memory timeline. S, it is okay to open your eyes now." Helper, as this occurs, release the new history anchor and go on with these last steps.

(24)   Step 24: This will be an excellent time to hug one another for a job well done. When ready, tell your S, "We will do the same thing for each of those parts of you that were abused."

Note 1: Helper, if you have to take a break, ensure that all parts that came out are invited back into their respective timelines. Let them know we will get back together to continue the process at another time. At that time, we will start at Part 2.b.(1) Step 1 when you are ready to continue.

Note 2: If you are continuing on, go back to Part 2.b.(4) Step 4 on page 100 and repeat the process for each younger part. Continue through step 24 until all the hurtful events and the associated hurt selves have a new history and experienced how life would have evolved differently.

Note 3: Then, once all memories have been rewritten, proceed with following the instructions for closing the session, Step 25.

(25) Step 25: Helper, say this, "Let's make sure all the parts that were invited out are back safely in their respective timelines. If all is in order, let them know we thank them all for their help in rewriting

each of the memories. These changes are for you to keep. We love each of you. Open your eyes now."

c. **Say to your S, "Take time to reflect on this process of creating new memories and the implications for your future."**

d. **Helper, discuss with your S and comment on what this experience has been like for both of you. Once all has been shared, go on.**

3. **Embracing the new history and preparing for the future.**

   a. **Assuring the younger parts that the new memories and related learnings are for them to keep.**

      (1) Once all the scenes have been rewritten, ask your S to speak to all the parts with the new memories, "To all these parts of me with the new histories, I assure you they are for you to keep and use as we move forward. I believe life for us is already better now, and I have lots of hope for this to continue as we keep growing and building on these new experiences."

      (2) When this reality has been absorbed, ask for a comment from your S. Ask, "What has this total experience been like? What now comes to mind that you could not have imagined before?" Listen to your S's response then go on.

   b. **Time for involving these new learnings in the future.**

      (1) Helper, say to your S, "Close your eyes and go inside. As you think about your new history with different choices and new outcomes at important junctures in life, can you imagine what it will be

like as we take these new learnings into the future from this day on?" Once your S has pondered this, Helper, say, "Open your eyes now and let's talk together about what comes to mind concerning the future."

c. **It is a great time for a celebration.**

(1) Helper, say to your S, "We deserve to celebrate this incredible accomplishment. The old, abusive memories are not running the show any longer. I welcome you to your new life and a new world. In the work of the next chapter, we will rehearse taking these new learnings into your future. That is exciting in itself, but let's enjoy this moment now. What do you think?" Listen to the S, then go on.

(2) Helper, you might have arranged for a birthday cake with seven candles or something similar to mark a new beginning for his or her new life. Enjoy a break to have some light fun together.

CLOSE FOR THE S

Helper, say to your S as you finish with the celebration and this session, "Congratulations again. Thank you for allowing me to be your guide through this recovery journey. You have made some incredible accomplishments, especially in this last segment. Wow! You re-wrote the old painful script/scripts and replaced it/them with memories full of life and personal freedom. I am excited to walk with you through the rest of this process too."

CLOSE FOR THE HELPER

Helper, this same praise goes to you too. You have just navigated through an incredibly important process of change work. The images that have continued to be a source of plague to your S have been dulled if not totally erased. The former impact has been effectively eliminated. A new life is now more possible than ever before. You have just attained another set of life-giving skills. Let me assure you that your value in the recovery community just increased dramatically. What is also exciting is that we are not finished yet, but we are getting oh, so close.

Close your eyes as you return back in your mind's eye to those woods and the fast-moving stream you are in the process of crossing. Notice the bank is really getting closer. Just four more main rocks to step onto and you will be finally stepping up onto the bank that used to be so distant. Now, let us concentrate on getting onto this next rock. As before, extend your leg as you plant your hiking boot safely onto this next rock. Then, shift your weight allowing you to safely plant your other leg onto this next rock. Reach your hand out to give your partner help to also step onto this rock next to you. You can now imagine that soon you will be able to step up onto what was this far bank and you will soon be able to walk normally, confidently and comfortably on dry land as you continue on to your destination. Now, let this image begin to fade as you open your eyes.

Only three more powerful chapters ahead in this incredible journey of recovery. Move on to Chapter Eight when you are ready.

Chapter Eight
Bringing the New Learnings into the Future

"I am convinced that all people can grow. It is a matter of connecting them with their inner resources. That is the therapeutic task."

—Virginia Satir

INTRODUCTION

Helper, you have been doing an incredible job of guiding your S to this point. Here is where all of the previous work will reap dividends as it is applied to future practice and rehearsal. This part reminds me of the movie *Back to the Future* starring Michael J. Fox. It was about time travel in a specially equipped car. The movie makes one think about how the past influences the future. So, on this part of the journey, you will be challenged to reach even higher in your skills of using imagination to effect powerful and lasting change. These skills will build on those you have already learned.

In this chapter, you will guide your S from appreciating the changes that have been made to his or her past history as a steppingstone to making improvements in behavior in some future event. Your S will be invited to find an upcoming event to rehearse in two ways, watching it then moving into the role.

Helper, I know as we get closer to the end of this journey, you will continue doing an excellent job of leading your S compassionately and artfully through these next steps by giving instructions which will include setting and releasing anchors (physical touches to the wrist).

1. Preparing for the primary tasks of this chapter.

    a. Review all the changes you created along with the new impact.

        (1) As before, say to your S, "Close your eyes and go inside. As you do, take time to review all the changes you created and put in place in your new history. I will activate the anchor we set as you made all these changes. This was referred to as your 'New History' change anchor. This will be anchor #1." (Helper, as best you can, activate this anchor in the place that it was set before.)

        (2) Continue saying, "Consider the ramifications of these changes to include new choices and pathways you could have made. Be aware of how your younger selves would mature and change as they became filled with the freedoms and qualities that your Precious Child had. Bring this review up to date as you could have grown into adulthood. Bring it up to this very day. When you sense that you have finished and appreciate the impact that comes from the new memories you put in place, let me know."

        (3) Helper, as you get a sign that your S is done, release the anchor #1 and say, "Open your eyes. Let me know what that was like. What was it like to review how differently life could have gone even up to this very day?" Once you have listened and responded, go on.

b. **Find an up-coming event to rehearse.**

(1) Helper, say to your S, "Now close your eyes and go inside. Ask all of your creative resources to help you search into the near future for some upcoming event that might need some attention and maybe even benefit from a dress rehearsal. It might be an event which you have not handled so well in the past. Or it could be something new you will be called on to do or something coming from inside yourself, a challenge that you want to perfect. Take time to find an event that meets one of these criteria. It could be some situation that you would like to handle better or something new you are being asked to do. It could be something you have marked off for yourself to do differently than in the past. Once you have found such a future event, open your eyes and let me know what you found." Helper, listen then ask, "What are the challenges this event presents for you?" When the interchange is complete, go on.

c. **Bring up the details of this event.**

(1) Helper, instruct your S by saying, "As before, close your eyes and go inside. As you are ready, bring up this scene you have discovered. Imagine the details the best you can guess about how it will most likely begin, where it will take place, who will be present and how will this feel for you. As before, place this beginning scene on hold or pause. Look around and get acquainted with where you are, who might be present, what time of day it is, what sounds might you hear, how you will be dressed, what will the weather/temperature/humidity be and anything else that helps you get oriented to this upcoming situation."

    (2) "It would be a good time to ask yourself if there are any resources you will need to carry out this upcoming event. Take all the time you need to prepare for putting the expected scene in motion. Let me know when you are finished setting the stage."

    (3) Helper, when you get the signal, say, "Open your eyes. What is the setting of the scene you have on pause? What is being asked of you or are you asking of yourself?" Helper, listen and once the interchange is complete, go on to 2.

2. Watching the future scene and then moving into the role as a dress rehearsal.

a. Watching the future scene.

    (1) Helper, say to your S, "It is time now for you to close your eyes and place the beginning scene on pause as before. This is where you believe the future scene will start. Get access to any resources you need to run this scene."

    (2) Tell your S, "When you are ready, I will set anchor #2 as you watch this scene unfold just the way you want it to go." (Helper, set anchor # 2.) "Now let the beginning unfold just the way you want it. Watch the future event as you work through the beginning, the middle, and then move toward the end. If you want to re-do any part, back up and do it over. Keep working on it until you get it just right. Let me know when you are finished." Helper, when you get the signal, release the anchor and say to your S, "Open your eyes. Let me know what transpired." When the interchange is complete, go on.

b. **The Dress Rehearsal: Moving through the scene by rehearsing it.**

(1) Helper, say to your S, "This time you get to step into the scene as if you are actually in it with your body. In this one you will not be watching yourself. In this rehearsal, it will be like you would be putting on a sweater, a blouse, or a shirt to try it on for size. In a moment, I will be asking you to step into the scene you just watched. I will set #3 anchor and keep it activated to represent the one you are now living out. It will be like a dress rehearsal in a stage play. I will add anchor #3 for the rehearsed scene in which you will be living or trying on the role. Go back to the beginning and put it on pause as before. When you are there let me know."

(2) Helper, as you get the signal, note that you are going to activate anchor #3 and hold it as your S has the scene on pause. Continue on by saying, "Now imagine you are stepping into this new scene (Helper, activate anchor #3) looking through your eyes, hearing your voice. See your hands and feet moving in your field of vision as you proceed through the scene. S, place yourself into this scene as if you are wearing your role. As you walk through this dress rehearsal and live out your role, I will continue to activate anchor #3. (Helper, continue to hold anchor #3.) Keep working through the beginning and the middle of the scene until you get to the end. As before, you can back up and re-do any part of it until you get it just right. If you like what you experienced, let me know." As you get the signal, Helper,

ask S, "What was that like?" Release the new anchor #3. Finish the interchange, then go on.

c. Blending the new rehearsed scene into the new history memories in two steps.

(1) Now, we will blend the rehearsed version (Anchor #3) with the one you created and watched (Anchor #2) until only the rehearsed one remains. Then, once this is complete, we will blend the rehearsed version into the original anchor #1, which will then connect the new rehearsed behavior to your new history. Anchor #3 will then be the extension of your new history.

(2) Helper, say, "As you close your eyes and go back inside, put the beginning scenes of the two versions on pause and let me know when you are ready. I will activate anchor #3 and #2 as you work through the entire scenes by running both of them simultaneously. When you are finished and you like your response with no need for changes, take the time to let Anchor #3 blend with #2 until #3 becomes #2 and #2 disappears. When that has occurred, let me know. Once you get an indication that anchor #3 is now blended into anchor #2, we will move on."

(3) Tell your S, "I will add anchor #1 with the new #3 activated. As I hold #1 and #3 together, let #3 blend into and become #1. This will connect the one you rehearsed in the future, become a part of your new history and be an extension of it. Let me know when this is complete." Once you get the nod that this has been completed, move on.

(4) Helper, release both anchors and say to your S, "This change is now attached and connected to

your new history. Open your eyes. This is a great, great accomplishment. This new tool will serve you well." Helper, ask S, "Well, what was that like for you?" Listen and respond as appropriate.

3. **Reflecting on the benefits from the Chapter 8 experience.**

   a. **This brings you and the S full circle.**

      (1) This journey started with you guiding the S through the steps of dealing with feelings. You set the stage for your S meeting his/her Precious Child and the hurt parts. Then you moved on to identifying the details of the abusive events. The S experienced taking back what was lost and giving up what did not belong in his/her body (The Exchange). This was followed by confronting and then forgiving the offender(s). Then, you directed the process of rewriting the abusive events. Finally, you introduced the methods of how to take all of this new learning into the future through the creative skills of imagination.

      (2) Helper, you have been through this journey every step of the way with your S. It has been an emotional roller coaster filled with new feelings, skills and experiences. Take a moment to go through this journey with your S. Each step laid the foundation for the next experience. Praise your S for doing so well and for hanging in there when it was not easy. The recovery journey is not an easy cakewalk, but it is worth every new step taken, no matter how difficult. Helper, in your own words, relay this to your S.

b. **The Dress Rehearsal makes the delivery easier.**

(1) Further, explain this to your S: "Research and experience have repeatedly demonstrated that because of the rehearsal practice, you will find it easier to enact the new changes." Alert your S, "When you step into the future scene, in real time, it will feel different because of the rehearsal. It is as if you have been there before. Which in a way is true. You have been there in the rehearsal."

(2) Helper, say, "Be aware that you can use the method for rehearsing, in imagination, any behavior in which you desire to improve or develop. The beauty is that you can do it anywhere. Your subconscious will get the idea of what you are wanting. All you need to do is to shut your eyes and go inside. This is the root behind the experience of sensing you have been there when you are in the situation in which you wish to apply the new learning. At one level you have been there. Enjoy this new learning experience and skill."

c. **You can make instantaneous changes wherever you are even if you are in the middle of some particular act or behavior sequence.**

(1) Continue explaining to your S "You can become pretty proficient with making changes 'on the fly,' so to speak. All you have to do is take a split second to shut your eyes and imagine the change, then do it. The action to correct or create a new response is basically the dress rehearsal we practiced before. It may seem to you like a long time being inside, but in reality, with practice it can be about as long as it takes to snap your fingers. Someone in your presence may notice that

you did something different. Of course, you will know exactly what you did. You can say something like, 'Just went inside for a moment to check something out.' Or you can say, 'I am not sure what,' or you can say nothing at all. Either way is quite okay."

(2) "This is a good reminder that this is your recovery. You do not owe anyone an explanation about the changes you have made or how you have done it. Reality is that if you tried to explain it, others would tend not to believe you anyway or not understand what you said."

CLOSE FOR THE S

"Let me tell you, S, you have done one incredible piece of work again. My hat is off to you. I salute you. I hold you high on the mountaintop. You are totally awesome. What an incredible walk into a great recovery." Recognize to your S that he/she completed this part of the program with flying colors. Now we will be moving into the final chapters. I will be turning over more of your recovery to you as I help equip you to keep growing.

CLOSE FOR THE HELPER

a. Helper, what an incredible journey for you. You have elevated your skill level to one that is now off the charts. What greater gift to be able to give to a struggling S than to show him or her how to discover and confront the painful details of the early hurts. Then to assist your S in standing up to offenders and getting things straight while speaking his or her truth. No one would believe you now have the ability to not only change one's history, but then turn right around and assist the S to take these learnings into the future. Triple wow!

b. Two more chapters to go through, my friend. The next chapter will focus on placing the future of the recovery work into the hands of the S. The primary message will be to do what it takes to keep it growing. The last chapter is a call to expansion and greatness for you.

c. Now as before, close your eyes and in your mind's, eye bring the scene from the stream in the woods back in focus. Be aware that you are almost across the stream. A few more steps and you will be actually walking onto that close bank soon. Look at the next rock. Keep your focus. Imagine placing your foot onto the next rock as you bring the other leg along with your weight shift to the point now that you are stable on this next rock. Reach out your hand to help your partner to step onto the rock with you. Once you both are stable on this new rock, take a moment before you let go of this scene, to be aware how far you two have come. Now there are just two more rocks to navigate across to finally being able to step onto the dry land.

Let the scene fade out as you open your eyes. When ready, move onto Chapter Nine.

Chapter Nine
No Options – Keep Growing

*"To become whole is to realize that
we are capable of peace and
understanding of ourselves and
others."*

—Caldwell C. Nichols

INTRODUCTION

Helper, you have done an incredible job getting your S to this point in his/her journey of recovery. It is essential to keep your S moving forward from here on their own. While a great deal has been accomplished, it is vital that your S keep using the tools and heeding the suggestions below. It would be a tragedy to risk going backwards after so much hard work and hard-earned progress has been achieved. I believe that you have planted some unquenchable fires, and a thirst for more learning, inside your S. This is because of your patience and your caring guidance. I commend you for a job well done by being a powerful, steadfast role model.

1. **It is a delicate victory for the S.**

   a. Helper, say to your S, "The recovery you have achieved is awesome and just short of a miracle. Because you are so early into the process, I cannot impress on you enough that it is a delicate victory. You have been a great trooper in this battle. Old habits, even with the enlightenment of the changes you have created for yourself, can slowly creep back in. The best protection you can set in motion for yourself is to continue to use the tools you have learned. In addition, it is imperative that you keep adding to this new learning and pressing on towards more growth."

b. Helper, continue by saying to your S, "One powerful way to continue the momentum is to be with others dedicated to learning and personal growth. This could be achieved by attending self-help groups or taking classes to improve your saleable skills. You could benefit from developing the habit of reading daily from a positive self-talk book. There are many good ones available."

c. Say to your S, "Appendix F of this book provides a list of helpful statements, affirmations and positive self-talk that you can take advantage of."

d. "This guide offered several thoughts in the text worthy of being reviewed regularly. I encourage you to select a few that really speak to you from whatever source and seriously consider posting the most significant ones in some prominent place, like on your bathroom mirror."

e. Helper, continue by saying, "The point is to keep alive the skills and concepts introduced here. It could be like taking time to go inside to check on your Precious Child and the other parts of you that were healed of the effects of the abusive acts. This could include using your imagination to rehearse some behaviors you desire to improve on like you did in the exercises in Chapter 8."

2. **Keep the subconscious active.**

a. In the beginning, new learning requires conscious effort.

(1) Helper, say to your S, "In the beginning, new learning requires some dedicated, conscious efforts. In time, as you have practiced the behaviors enough, it becomes easier. This lessening of the need for conscious effort is a strong clue that some things are beginning to be controlled by your subconscious. The subconscious functions differently than the conscious mind. It works a little slower and requires several or many repetitions until it 'gets' what is desired. So, any time you add new behaviors or skills, be patient with yourself. The more the subconscious takes over, the more your conscious mind will eventually be left with additional time to work on other things."

(2) Helper, continue: "Let me give you an example of this process, which comes from the annals of physiological psychology and the concept of accommodation. The experimenter placed glasses on the subjects that reversed their fields of vision. What was actually up appeared down. What was down appeared to be up. So, as they moved their hands or feet, these appeared in the upper part of their vision. Over time, they began to function fairly effectively with the prisms that reversed the field of vision still on. The subjects reported that they did not know when it actually occurred, but it happened gradually. They had made the reverse inside themselves such that what was up seemed actually up and what was down appeared down or in the lower part of their visual field. This is a perfect example of the subconscious processes eventually taking over."

b. Helper, say, "It goes without much thought that eating healthy, getting regular sleep, and participating in regular exercise is good for you.

Similarly, picking friends who give you energy, not drain you, because they are taking good care of themselves too. Those are the ones you want to include in your close circle of friends."

c. Helper, continue saying, "Get in the habit of taking time to practice self-relaxation skills. After several times, your subconscious will get the idea of what you are wanting. The goal is to achieve a total state of relaxation from head to toe, including your mind. You can do this just about anywhere. You begin by shutting your eyes, going inside and consciously relaxing your tendons and muscles all the way around and through from your head, face, neck your arms, body, legs and feet. Eventually, it will take just seconds to achieve a full and total state of relaxation."

3. Manage your time and boundaries well.

a. Helper, say to your S, "It is vital to set reasonable boundaries for yourself."

(1) Helper, continue on, "Part of setting good boundaries is to allow time for productive time, but also for relaxation, social time, and quiet time as needed. There are a couple of rules here to note about balance. One is that if you have been alone for many hours, like when writing a report, then schedule time with others. The flip side of this rule is that if you have had a great deal of contact with people, then plan for some alone time for yourself."

(2) Helper, say, "The other boundary concerns the making of your daily to-do list. The number of items on the list needs to be reasonable in length so they generally can be completed in one day. I am aware that some items may be longer projects that take several days or weeks. A certain part may be allocated

for that project over time. It took the author several years to come up with 6 as his manageable number of items. Generally, he completes them in a day and rarely misses the goal now. With the list being manageable, this allows for the unexpected thing that may require attention but was unplanned. A manageable list allows for this to be handled with reasonable effort. If your list is wearing you out, change it immediately. The author used to be a slave or a hostage to his formerly long lists. This is a quote from the author: 'I laughed at myself when it occurred to me that I accomplished more from having a manageable list rather than pushing to complete an impossible one. I can remember that moment when I literally asked myself, why did I not make this simple change before now?'"

b. Helper, say to your S, "Make sure you arrange time for pleasurable activities and social time with people and events that cause you to laugh. Laughter is truly good medicine. This includes spending time with those people who energize you. Stay away from those who drain you. It's nothing against some, but it is your life and recovery. Who you spend time with either builds you up and energizes you or tears you down. So, who do you pick? A companion to this is that the author strongly encourages you to join a support group. The point of this is to be with others who value personal growth. Incorporating these ideas into our daily life is just smart personal management."

c. Helper, read to your S, "People forget how rewarding it is to your spirit and soul to donate time to volunteer. This is especially true when you are engaged in processing heavy experiences like you have been. Some spend lovely time caring for animals at shelters, joining a Habitat for Humanity house building project, or helping with a benefit bike ride. The cause you give to is not as important as just doing it. This is a great gift to the one on the receiving end as well as to the one giving his or her time. This is a win-win-win situation."

CLOSING REMARKS

Helper, this completes the more formal part of this program. You decide how you want to close out this session with your S. I trust you will know just the right way to do that. Once you have completed closure with your S, read on. The remainder of the material is for you and your dreams. Let go of what you were doing, modeling and teaching this material with compassion and patience with your S. Clear your mind of that process as you prepare for the information and challenges presented in the next chapter. Hopefully, this is just the beginning for you. My friend, you successfully completed this journey with your S. Now, it is time to focus on what is possible for you.

As before, close your eyes and return in your mind's eye to those woods and the stream you have been moving across, from rock to rock. Be aware there is just one more rock separating you from the bank. Note how far you have come. You remained dry by being patient and careful as you navigated onto the next rock. The balancing of your weight was absolutely perfect as you trusted one another to shift your balance and your footing just at the right time and way. As before, plant your foot onto this last rock. Once you are stable, reach out to your partner with your outreached hand. So gently help him/her step off the rock onto the one you are standing on. Take note of the beauty of nature the woods provides as you come close to being able to continue on down the path ahead. Now let those images fade as you begin to open your eyes.

When you are ready, continue on to Chapter Ten.

Chapter Ten
What a Ride! What a Guide!

*"The greatest reward may not be
one's achievements; it may be what
we become along the way."*

—*Gary J. Butler, Ph.D.*

INTRODUCTION

You made it through! Welcome. Let's face it. This has not been an easy journey, but you have hung in there. You walked side by side with your S while he or she shared painful memories. Without question, you have convinced me that you have the heart to do this work. Welcome. I cannot tell you how wonderful it feels to have another joining in with others who are aware of the great need for trained people in this area.

I feel joy as I am aware of a certain kinship with you just because you completed this sequence. I know that you have offered the level of care and compassion your S deserves. You have accepted him or her just as he or she is without judgment. You walked beside him/her through some of their dark and painful experiences as well as the victories. This translates into a sustaining, life-giving hope. This also translates into "Someone truly cares about me. There must be hope for me and my situation." What greater gift is there than giving a survivor the hope that things will continue to get better?

Even if you think that you may not have enough experience to offer services to other S's, let me assure you that it is what is in your heart that will go before you. This will open all the doors you need opened to reach out to more S's.

1. **A great time for reflection.**

   a. **You are beginning to separate yourself from the crowd.**

      (1) By working through this training, you are beginning to separate yourself from others. These others may say they can deal with ACE trauma survivors as if it's no big deal. But I am here to tell you that being trained to deal specifically with ACE survivors is a major deal. I have helped those survivors who went to one of those helpers with no focused training and it was apparent that they were not making any progress or at least slow progress. These skills which you are becoming familiar with are of high value for trauma survivors.

      (2) Depending on your future desires, these skills can take you to some pretty great places. But it is not just the training, it involves having the heart and compassion for the S's position. I am here to tell you that the sky is the limit in this field. You can go as high as you are willing to dream. It may be to assist a few Survivors becoming free, or it may eventually be to become known for training others.

   b. **Let's look at the major skills you have so courageously been embracing.**

      (1) In the beginning, you learned the vital importance of an S being able to identify the kinds of abuse

he/she had experienced. Your S was then asked to expand on the description of the abuse(s). Next, you focused on naming one's feelings. You helped identify the S's ability to name and talk about feeling states.

A method for differentiating between two formats, *I feel_____ versus I feel like _____* was explained. A way to discern one's primary feeling words (PFWs) was presented for those who had difficulty in naming different feeling states and associated words.

(2) Your Ability to direct the use of imagination has been awesome.

(a) You truly began to open the personal discovery of what happened to the S by a review in imagination of the details of the abusive events. You also supported your S completing the answering of detailed questions about the hurtful events. The details were recorded on the Master List of Abusive Events (MLAE) sheets. Most importantly, your assistance aided your S in putting his or her story together. Typically, this sharing is the first time the S has shared these sensitive and delicate details with anyone.

(b) You guided the S through finding his/her Precious Child and those younger parts that were hurt.

(c) With your able support, your S stood up for his or herself when confronting his or her offender(s) by applying the gift of imagination. Then your S completed the "exchange" of getting back what was lost and giving up what he or she had been carrying that did not belong any longer in his or her spirit. I know you saw a dramatic change in your S as he or she experienced his/her personal power come forth from this process of standing up to his or her offender(s) speaking the truth about what had happened.

(d) You took the next step again in using imagination to lead your S in forgiving his or her offender(s). This segment ended with the S experiencing forgiving him or herself.

(e) In addition, visualization was utilized in changing the memories and to plan for up-coming events through a two-step process of watching then trying on the new behaviors. You assisted your S to re-write his/her history. This was to defuse the impact of the early painful memories. Lastly, imagination was presented for the S to take the new learning into future events. You guided him or her from watching the planned scene and also encouraged the S to rehearse it as if he or she were in his or her own body, moving through the sequences of the anticipated scene. What Survivors typically report is an amazement of how easy it is to bring the new planned behaviors into the new future event. This is an example of the power of the "rehearsal" in imagination.

(3) You closed out this guided journey by encouraging your S to keep using the skills taught and strongly advised him or her to attend self-help groups.

(a) The point being is that you strongly advised your S to be around people who treasure personal growth. You offered suggestions about keeping good boundaries and tips on effective daily planning. One other simple habit to carry out daily involves the reading of positive affirmations like those included in Appendix F.

(b) Putting together these suggestions may be as significant and have as great an impact as all the steps your S took along this journey to achieve a start to a great recovery. If there is no commitment to keep the learning progressing, then the S risks slowly losing what has been gained. Experience has shown that old habits eventually go away to the degree that new behaviors continue to be utilized to replace them.

(4) In the beginning you truly began to open the personal discovery of what happened to the S by a review of the categories of abuse that happens to children at the hands of their offenders. You also supported your S making brief notes as he or she learned about the categories of abuse and safely encouraged him or her to make it personal. Most importantly, your assistance aided your S in putting his or her story together.

c. The sky is the limit.

(1) I am saying that because the need is so great for trained people to be available for individual or group consultations, I strongly encourage you to be brave. Be willing to take the risk to continue your own growth and development in this field. I have found the work tremendously rewarding, as people get hope from coming face to face with their Precious Child or experiencing the relief that occurs during the "exchange" with the offenders. Assisting an S in becoming free of the bondage of the early abuse is worth its weight in gold. It does not get any better than this.

3. What to do now.

a. Give serious consideration for your future in this field.

(1) Each person's interests and situations vary, but I encourage you to seriously contemplate your plans about what you might consider doing from here. You may have worked through this guide out of curiosity, or you may be a graduate student looking for a topic for a dissertation. You might also be a professional in the helping professions seeking to focus your practice in this area. You could be part of a group desiring to start an in-patient or out-patient treatment program. I have something to offer for any dream you are willing to dream. I am here to listen to whatever you are contemplating and assist in giving your dreams wings for flight.

(2) As a minimum, I strongly encourage you to write down what you are considering. Put the list aside for a few days, then re-visit it. At that time make

a decision about what you want to get serious about. If you are almost ready to pop with excitement, I for sure would like to be a part of your planning. The skills you have now been introduced to are just the beginning. But what a beginning, whatever your goals are.

b. The possibilities are endless.

(1) It is an incredible time to get involved in this field. This is especially true in light of what is happening in our society today. There are some strong movements that are gaining momentum to confront abuse, not just of children but of adults in every situation imaginable. Women abused by men of status and power are speaking up with a united voice. For example, the USA gymnasts who were abused by a "team" doctor for years and years, in spite of complaints being reported to authorities. They are no longer willing to let the carried shame silence them. They were, and in some cases are, victims who are finding their collective voices as Survivors. Consider for a moment the victims of school shootings and the growing movement to stand for change. The veils of denial are coming off in many sectors—government, education, the military, business, Hollywood, sporting fields, and churches, to name a few.

(2) For your planning, it is just the beginning of several powerful movements. This "hidden epidemic" of ACE survivors is part of this as more are coming out, about the impact of early abuse in their lives. Whether you want to lead a few S's a year through this recovery

program or become a well-known voice for this movement, I believe the timing could not be better for getting involved. Come on in. As you look back later, I know you will be so glad you did.

(3) All it takes is your decision to keep growing from here. You are having a great start in your skill development right now. All you need to do is commit to developing a plan for moving ahead. If you feel a bit or a large degree of fear, that is good. If you are not experiencing some fear, then I believe you are not dreaming big enough.

All the resources you need are available. Additional information and resources can be found on my Facebook page: **"Becoming Free"**.

Please contact me for consultation by email:

Butlergl1060@gmail.com

"There is no greater victory than to be a part of leading a survivor into a new life of recovery, free of the impact of early abuse."

—*Gary J. Butler, Ph.D.*

Post-script: *"Close your eyes with me. I can see the steppingstones that you took crossing the fast-moving water of this stream. The bank you stepped off of looks to be so far away now. Your next challenge is to step off this last rock and step up onto this bank. As before, place your boot onto this bank and then transfer your weight. Stand up so that you are stable with both feet on dry ground. Bend down and help your partner up onto the bank beside you. Take a final look around at the woods and all of the gorgeous nature in this area: the trees, the light breezes, the beams of sunlight bouncing about, the tweets of the birds and the white sound of that rushing water. As you turn away from the water, you see the path leading deeper into the woods. I am right here ready to walk with you each step of the way. It has been a great journey. I believe there are many more*

If you found this book helpful, I would really appreciate a short review. Your help in spreading the word is highly valued and reviews make it much easier for readers to find the book.

Also, by Gary Butler:

Amazon Link:

https://tinyurl.com/4tv53sye

Appendix A
A Tool For Discovering Primary Feeling Words

INTRODUCTION

This Appendix is offered as a supportive tool to the material in Chapter 2: Identifying and Expressing Feelings. In that chapter, it is acknowledged that early on in recovery most Survivors struggle to identify feelings. At some level, they know that they need to learn more about how to express them appropriately and constructively.

The section below explains the steps to discovering what we will call the Primary Feeling Words, or PFWs for short. These are the eight Primary Feeling Words from which hundreds of others are derived: joy, pain, anger, shame, guilt, fear, loneliness, and sadness. The point is to begin to identify all the feelings and become familiar with calling them by name. This becomes a grounding or centering experience that you will seek to repeat. It might take several PFWs to capture what one of those you may be feeling. For instance, you can be so lonely that you could feel pain and also feel sadness. Similarly, you can love someone to such a degree that if someone else does something that causes that loved one pain, you might experience pain and anger too. Sometimes the word you choose may have many different meanings and, in some situations, there is an absence of an English word. For instance, the word "love" in the English language can be used to mean affection, admiration, liking, or refer to a committed, unbending love for someone, no matter what that person might do. The Greek word for this kind of committed, unbending and unending love is agape. It is interesting to note that there is not an equivalent word for this in English.

Most people use thoughts, phrases, or adjectives in an attempt to identify their feelings. Typically, it takes the form of "I feel like_____." What comes in the blank is a thought, a phrase, a noun, an adverb, or an adjective, but rarely a PFW. An example would be, *"I feel like I am accepted."* What PFW might be behind this report of being accepted? It would be joy. So, if we put this together, it would be that to feel "accepted" would be an attempt to express the PFW, to feel joy. This is explained in more detail next.

The Process of Identifying Primary Feeling Words (PFWs)

1. When you think about an experience in which you desire to discover what you may be feeling, pick a word or phrase that begins to define your experience. Pick whatever comes to mind first.

2. Next, ask yourself if you picked one of the PFWs. Then, if you did, you have conquered the first stage of recovering your feelings. You can then complete the sentence, "I feel_____." The PFW or words go in the blank. If you did not select a PFW, then slowly go through the list of eight primary feeling words and ask yourself which one or combination of PFWs fit the best. Since there are many words or phrases possible that you could pick to express your feelings, the list offered below will make it easier to identify the PFW's.

3. A list is offered below. These can be words from which you can begin to discover the eight PFWs listed

above. This is not intended to be an exhaustive compilation, but these are listed as an illustration of the process. Note that potential PFWs that create the particular word will be in the parentheses that follow each word. The letters will be as follows: "J" for joy, "P" for pain, "A" for anger, "Sh" for shame, "G" for guilt, "F" for fear, "L" for lonely and "Sd" for sad.

4. Feeling numb is a special circumstance. This generally indicates that one is feeling a lot of intense emotions that have typically been present for an extended period of time but have not been named or spoken. Once one has identified the core Primary Feeling Words and expressed them, that "numbness" tends to go away.

5. Like the example in the introduction presented above, here is another one of how to use the list below in the process of discovery. Name your feeling word or words. You may or may not find it in the list below. If it is not a PFW, then think of your experience and slowly repeat each of the PFWs to yourself. Note the one or ones that fit or feel right inside. Let's say you feel you were abandoned. You might say, "I feel like I am abandoned." Since it is not a PFW, go through the eight PFWs until you find which PFWs "fit." In the list below, you can see that P, A, F, L could be possibilities for your specific PFWs that created or could be behind an experience of being abandoned.

6. When you discover "that fit," note what it is like internally as you name the Primary Feeling Word(s) that are "right" for you. You will tend to have an experience of peace or tranquility as you discover the one or ones that is or are the best "fit." This is your personal internal signal that this is your PFW (or

words). These PFWs define your feeling experience and are not up for debate. Then you can put this all together and say, "I have a sense of being abandoned, and this leaves me feeling pain, anger, fear, and lonely."

An expanded list of feeling-word possibilities or words that will get you to your PFWs:

Abandoned (P, A, F, L)

Abused (P, A, Sh, F)

Accepted (J)

Admired (J)

Affection (J)

Affirmed (J)

Aggravated (A)

Aggressive (J, A, F)

Alone (A, F, L, P, Sd)

Anxious (P, F)

Appreciated (J)

Betrayed (P, A, F, L, Sd)

Blamed (P, A, L, Sh, G)

Bored (A, L, Sd)

Calm (J)

Caring (J, L, Sd)

Cautious (F)

Centered (J)

Cherished (J, P)

Comfortable (J)

Concern (P, F)

Confident (J)

Confused (P, A, F)

Content (J)

Curious (J, F)

Deceived (P, A, Sd)

Defensive (P, A, F)

Delighted (J)

Dependent (J, P, A, Sd)

Depressed (A, Sh, F, L, Sd)

Deserted (P, A, Sh, F, L, Sd)

Dirty (P, A, Sh, Sd)

Disappointed (P, A, Sd)

Disgusted (P, A, Sd)

Dizzy (P, Sh, F)

Drained (P, A, Sh, F)

Embarrassed (P, A, Sh)

Empowered (J, A)

Empty (P, F, Sd)

Enthusiastic (J) Excited (J)

Flexible (J)

Free (J)

Frustrated (A)

Happy (J)

Hate (P, A, F)

Helpless (P, A, F, Sd)

Hopeful (J)

Hopeless (P, A, F, L)

Hostile (P, A, Sh, F)

Hurt (P, A, F)

Important (J, A)

Inadequate (P, A, Sh, Sd)

Independent (J, A)

Insecure (P, A, F, L)

Irritated (A)

Isolated (P, F, L, Sd)

Joyous (J)

Justified (J, A)

Left out (P, A, L, Sd)

Love (J)

Loved (J)

Mad (P, A)

Manipulated (P, A, Sd)

Mischievous (J, A)

Misunderstood (P, A, L, Sd)

Naughty (A, Sh)

Negative (P, A, Sh, Sd)

Needed (J)

Nervous (F)

Nurture (J)

Nurturing (J)

Pleased (J)

Positive (J)

Possessive (J, A, F)

Powerful (J, A)

Powerless (J, P, Sd)

Precious (J)

Pressured (P, A)

Protective (J, F)

Protected (J)

Proud (J, A)

Qualified (J)

Rage (P, A, Sh, F)

Relaxed (J)

Relief (J)

Rejected (P, A, Sh, F, L, Sd)

Rested (J)

Satisfied (J)

Scared (F)

Secure (J)

Self-Doubt (P, F)

Serene (J)

Sexy (J, A, Sh)

Shameful (P, Sh, Sd)

Shock (P, F)

Shocked (P, A, F)

Shut out (P, A, Sh, F, L, Sd)

Shy (P, F, L, Sd)

Special (J)

Strong (J, A)

Stuck (A, P, L)

Sure (J)

Supported (J)

Surprised (J, F)

Sympathetic (J)

Tempted (Sh, G, F)

Tender (J, Sd)

Terrified (P, A, F)

Tired (P, Sh, Sd)

Trapped (P, A, L, Sd) Tuned-out (J, A)

Turned-off (P, A, Sd)

Turned-on (J, A)

Unimportant (P, Sh, L, Sd)

Unsure (P, Sh, F)

Uplifted (J)

Validated (J)

Valuable (J)

Valued (J)

Vulnerable (P, A, F, L)

Weak (P, Sh, F)

Welcome (J)

Worried (P, F)

Appendix B
Outreach Response Survey

_____ **Neglect:**

Primary care givers responsible for caring for someone who is unable to care for themselves fail to do so.

_____ **Abandonment:**

Primary care givers unavailable or left.

_____ **Physical Abuse:**

Beatings, hit with implements.

_____ **Sexual Abuse:**

Direct Contact or Indirect, Incest.

_____ **Intellectual Abuse:**

Ridiculing thoughts, talents, lack of stimulation or support.

_____ **Spiritual Abuse:**

By a clergy or member of a church

Any abuse is spiritual abuse.

_____ **Weird, bizarre, extreme violence:**

Cult rituals, bestiality, devil worship

_____ **Family Violence:**

Angry outburst, physical fights

Use of knives, guns as threats or actually used

Seeing/hearing evidence of violence

Blackened eyes, bruises, cuts, broken bones

Untreated alcoholism, drug abuse

Suicide attempts or suicidal thoughts

_____ Emotional/Psychological Abuse:

Called degrading names

Rigid or changing rules or no rules

No talk or family secrets

Truth distorted or denied

Incestuous triangles (child given favor at the exclusion of another adult)

If you checked 1 or more categories, do you believe this event, or these events impacted the quality of your life?

_____ Yes _____ No

If "Yes", did you seek help? _____ Yes _____ No

If "Yes", was it helpful? _____ Yes _____ No

Appendix C
Expanded Description of Types of Abuse

Expanded Description of the Types of Abuse:

1. Neglect.

Neglect is basically the inattention or inadequate attention to the basic needs of the child. Each child has a right to adequate access to food, clothing, personal hygiene, shelter, medical care, dental care, physical and emotional nurturing, guidance and information to help the child be successful in life. Topics could include but are not limited to sexual education information, how to dress, importance of who you spend time with, power of doing the right thing even when it is not easy, handling finances, and encouragement in how to develop one's own strengths.

a. Food and meals.

Food may not have been consistently available or little care exercised in preparing the meals adequately. Groceries might not have been available very often. Many times, Survivors have reported how often they had to fend for themselves by eating whatever they could find in the kitchen. Parents could have been unemployed, preoccupied, and inadequate or diverted by addictions or other personal and psychological problems. Food could have been a source of control or punishment. Admonitions like, "Eat it until it is gone. I paid good hard-earned money for that meal you do not seem to want to eat." Or, withholding food as a punishment like this, "You are not going to eat with us tonight young man for pulling that stupid stunt at school today. Forget eating tonight!" Sometimes the tensions are so high at dinnertime, the child is too upset to digest his or her food properly. He or she might be so upset to vomit up whatever was eaten. Digestion tends to not function correctly when one is in a flight or fight situation.

b. Clothing.

Clothing not being cleaned, not being available, not fitting or way out of style can be hurtful. At an elementary school in a small coastal town I lived in, I was appalled upon discovering how many children lived in tents in the woods with their families. At a quarterly awards program, you could pick out those children. Others had trouble being close to them because they were dirty and smelled bad. Their clothes were dingy. My granddaughter attended that school and when I asked about some of those kids, she wrinkled up her nose while saying it was hard to do things with them because of the foul odors. You can only guess at the hurtful burden these kids had to endure that they did not cause or ask for.

One man reported the pain he experienced from his highly rigid and abusive father who bought his clothes at secondhand stores. One year his dad purchased for the man, at the time a child, a pair of military style brogans. These are short top-heavy boots. Years later these came into vogue. At the time of this man's childhood, they were not in style. Kids at school teased him unmercifully. He lived on a Midwest dairy farm. Late one afternoon while heading back to the house from the fields, he waded across a swollen creek. The boot got stuck in heavy mud. He went on without the boot. Thinking he was finally rid of that boot; he went on to the house. Once his dad realized the boot was missing, he ordered the child to go out into the dark night without a light to recover the boot.

Clothes available could be hand-me-downs. That in and of itself is not a problem. But if the styles are out of date, the material is extremely faded, the items do not fit, or do not go together, it can be hurtful. Likewise, lack of guidance in what to wear can be a source of pain when other adults or children make fun of the Survivor's attire.

c. Lack of facilities.

A lack of facilities in which to bathe, to use the bathroom, or as simple as just not having soap available in which to wash oneself can lead to being unnecessarily embarrassed and hurt.

Closely akin to this would be inattention to giving advice on personal hygiene. This could be another source of pain.

d. A safe and predictable place to live.

A safe and predictable place to live should be available to all children. One Survivor reported coming home from school one day to find that her family had emptied out their home and left town without any warning or consideration of this Survivor's needs. Some Survivors have reported that several siblings had to share small or inadequate space for sleeping. With no consideration for male's or female's issues of sexual maturing and need for privacy, this can be another source of pain.

Some have reported living in squalor or moving from relative to relative or friends' places, which often meant changing schools so frequently there was little or no opportunity to develop friends or even have any continuity with teachers and classroom work. Adequate and stable shelter is necessary for the normal development of a child. Anything short of that can be abusive.

e. Medical and dental care.

Children have a right to adequate and reasonable medical and dental care. Because of monetary concerns or just neglect and mismanagement, regular checkups are not scheduled, immunization shots are missed, or appointments are cancelled with no intention of rescheduling them. Ongoing problems that get put off typically become worse. In one case, a Survivor had a hypochondriac for a parent and was taken to emergency rooms and different doctors and clinics continuously. This severely interrupted any kind of consistency in the child's life.

f. Physical and emotional nurturing.

Physical and emotional nurturing is vital for a child to thrive.

I have observed repeatedly that those who suffered horrendous abuse and by rights should have been totally disabled with severe psychological problems were fairly functional. I began to predict eventually what the answers would be, for upon inquiry, the responses were frequently consistent. In these cases, an aunt, a grandmother, or a family friend who knew what was happening to the child would give hugs and communicate their love. This would be treasured by the Survivor. It would be carried inside by the child as a warm fuzzy like an emotional, internalized version of a teddy bear. The message to the child was that things would get better and that even though times were tough now, he or she was still loveable. Receiving loving messages like this from someone who cares to say that one is loveable seems to literally be life giving. These expressions of love create lifelines of hope. It is like the message in the inspirational song, "Over the Rainbow." Past the storm clouds, there are blue skies waiting for you.

I found that those who did not receive this nurturing had more severe symptoms and their recovery tended to be more difficult. Below in the segment on abandonment, read about the classic psychological study of day care centers from WWII era. It serves as a powerful reminder of the significant role nurturing plays in an infant's survival.

I believe the connection to a child by a loving, caring adult is one of the ways that a child begins to know who he or she is. The direct and the non-verbal feedback over time communicates things such as, "You are loveable, capable, and have a great future before you." As the adult gets to know more about the child's strengths, these tend to get reinforced. This helps the child know more about who he or she is.

In some families, either because of chaos in the life of the family, diversions such as long hours working or drug and alcohol addictions and possibly other compulsive behaviors, this life-directing resource is withheld or unavailable to the child. Sometimes I have discovered that the pattern of care or the lack thereof is merely a repetition of the patterns the caregivers were exposed to as children. Therefore, some are just repeating how they were treated. Not that this is a justifiable excuse, but it does add to some understanding of how it happens.

On the other extreme is the parent or some other adult who becomes enmeshed with a child. This can include the child being made to be a surrogate mate or an adult attempting to live the life he or she never had through the child. The child tends to get a distorted view of who he or she is, or not reality based or at best a limited perspective at all.

Many years ago, I helped coach a little league baseball team. One player was an exceptionally small kid. His dad had been stationed in Germany in the military. While in that country, one of the guys the dad was stationed with had been a pitcher in the minor leagues. He had this fellow work with his young son. The dad kept assertively reminding us that we needed to put his son in as pitcher. We never answered him directly.

In one game, one of our pitchers we had worked with became sick during the game. We were limited to how many innings you can play the kids. The one who had been pitching had reached his limit on innings he could pitch. We had no one else we thought could pitch. So, we were in a bind. Against my strong objection, the other coach told the dad we would put his son in as pitcher. The kid could not throw the ball to the batter's plate after several attempts. Of course, the kid tried his hardest. So, we had to pull him out. As predicted, the kid was dejected even though we hugged him and made it clear we knew he had done his best. We and the team let him know we were proud of him for trying. The kid who was upset at first began shaking it all off and got back into supporting the team from the bench.

The dad proceeded to get behind the chain link fence right behind the kid and yell at the top of his lungs how embarrassed he was by his son's poor performance. The young boy began to slump over and lowered his head as his eyes started to fill with tears. I felt awful for this young child. As they were leaving, the dad continued to berate him and verbally beat his son up. Just watching that incident bothered me for weeks after that. I can only imagine the impact that dad had on that kid with the father being so unrealistic about his son's abilities.

Several years ago, I met a young man who had some serious problems getting his life going. I had an occasion to be present when his mother came up to him. She did what I call "oohed and gooed" on him by talking to him as if he were a small child. She spoke to him using pet names for him. Then she placed a big wet lingering kiss on his lips and gave him a full body hug. It took everything inside of me not to vomit.

This is not to blame her for her actions because the adult son has to be the one to recognize what is going on. He has to be the one to begin to set healthy boundaries leading to a break away from the blurred role of what could be termed his "mother-wife." Until he does, the odds are stacked against him for having a chance at an independent life and to develop his unique strengths and skills.

My experience has shown me that children who are in such an enmeshed relationship with a parent tend not to handle the empowerment well. It is like handing over the keys to a powerful car to an inexperienced teen driver. It is not unusual for these children to expect that the world meet all their demands.

Family therapists have labeled these as "King Babies." This is one of those situations that would not invite an investigation by authorities but could be experienced by the adult child as a hurt that is uncovered later in life.

g. Guidance and information.

Guidance and information sometimes for the Survivor was unavailable or presented in a distorted way. All children deserve to be educated about how to succeed in life. Topics include sexual maturity, building relationships, handling of finances, working through adversity, finding a career, planning for the future, and so forth. For some parents, for whatever the reason, they did not get it or just do not possess the information. These parents cannot give what they do not have. For others, they may tell off color jokes or give children misinformation. For instance, telling a sexually maturing teen they will go to hell if they masturbate can be hurtful.

2. Abandonment.

Abandonment is when a parent or primary caregiver is either emotionally or physically unavailable to attend to the child's needs. Sometimes it is both physical and emotional. It can be due to emotional problems or psychological ones such as a paranoid personality. Sometimes there can be extended periods of physical illness on the part of the caregiver(s). But even in those situations, the child deserves to be cared for in a safe and nurturing way.

Abandonment could be a passive-aggressive way of expressing anger at the child. Maybe the parent(s) harbor(s) resentment about the child being born and the obligations and responsibilities that come with parenting. These parents may have been abandoned too and acting out what had happened to them.

The importance of the availability of emotional nurturing cannot be over emphasized. A classic example of this need comes from a study conducted in the midst of WWII. The government began providing daycare facilities for those mothers who manned the factories and other places to support the war effort. One daycare center had a significantly higher infant death rate than other centers. Upon further inquiry, it was discovered the staff was smaller in the one center that was experiencing the increased death rate. Everything else was found to be the same. It was concluded that the babies were not being held enough. As staff numbers were increased and the babies were held more, that center's death rate came back down to match more of the other centers.

In summary, abandonment is literally that—leaving the child for extended times or permanently without adequate plans for physical or emotional care.

3. Physical abuse.

Physical abuse is usually what people think of first when thinking of child abuse. Sexual abuse might be their next thought. Physical abuse occurs when whippings become beatings. The use of implements such as a hair brush, lit cigarettes, a stiff board or stick that draws blood, razor straps, or metal clothes hangers stuck in ears or other body openings would be considered abusive. Slapping the face, beatings, banging the child's head, and hair pulling would be classified as physical abuse. Observing physical abuse of another adult or child hurts the child who observes these acts. To the child, it is like it is happening to him or her.

In one case, the father would read Bible verses to his three children while he demanded they be naked. He would then beat the Survivor and her two siblings with a leather belt. Being the oldest, the Survivor would try to position herself on top of her siblings to receive the blunt of the blows. She could not bear to see her brother and sister get beaten. She would feel the pain of any hurts inflicted onto her siblings by this abusive father.

4. Sexual abuse.

Sexual abuse can involve direct sexual contact or indirectly such as inappropriate innuendos or talk. It can be acts disguised as play such as tickling. In reality, the touch as play can involve brushing genitals, buttocks, breasts, or thighs, and cause sexual arousal on the part of the offender. It can come in the form of sexual thoughts toward a child. Sexual abuse can come to the child by observing sexual acts from which he or she needed to be protected.

Direct sexual acts perpetrated by a family member onto the child is called incest. This is distinguished from sexual acts on a child by a nonfamily member and are termed molestations. To be very specific, I will list direct acts of sexual abuse below and then the more indirect forms of sexual abuse. Both can be extremely hurtful.

a. Examples of direct acts of sexual abuse become incest if performed by a family member.:

1) Touching or fondling the child's private parts or asking the child to touch or fondle the adult's private parts.

2) Sensual or wet, maybe lingering, kisses with the child.

3) Sexual hugging so there is firm, full-body physical contact, especially in the chest and hip regions of bodies.

4) Engaging the child in oral sex, anal sex, sexual intercourse, fondling with fingers, objects, or sex organs.

5) The child being asked to masturbate the adult or the adult masturbating the child.

6) Forcing children to have sex with one another.

7) Lap sitting which makes child uncomfortable, especially if it arouses the adult.

8) Rape.

9) Flashing and exposing adult genitals to a child.

b. Examples of indirect sexual abuse:

1) Lack of appropriate boundaries in the home. It could be the child is exposed to sexual hugging and fondling between adults. This could include not shutting bedroom doors or not protecting them from bedroom sounds when adults are having sex. There could be an absence of modesty in dress, such as wearing skimpy night wear, underwear, or being nude in the presence of children over one year old.

2) Bringing the child into the marriage relationship. This could be by one parent sharing private especially sexual matters or other marital concerns with the child. One parent could encourage a strong relationship with one child. Names for that child can be a clue, such as, "My little princess," or "My little man." When the other parent is excluded from that relationship or the child is put above the other parent, then this can be abusive. One aspect of this is that it gives that child a power or an empowerment in the relationship that is not good for him or her. This is equivalent to handing the keys for the family car to a thirteen- year-old and saying, "take it." The point is that it is too much power for a child to handle.

3) Sometimes a generation above will reach down and build an unhealthy bond with a child that is used against the parents. This dynamic can be the set up for many forms of acting out or acting in later in life for the child if not during the time of childhood. If there are direct sexual acts or even sexual innuendos in these unbalanced triangle relationships, it is not unusual for the child or the adult child later to act out sexually in extreme or unhealthy ways.

4) Observing sexual abuse.

5) Shaming the child for being male or female and calling a child degrading names. This could be by ridiculing about size of body parts or lack of sexual development or healthy sexual development. Names like slut or whore, or "You will never be a man like me you wimp," can be hurtful.

6) Over-controlling of dating relationship to include grilling about sexual activities after a date.

7) Being aware of extra-marital affairs the adult(s) may be engaged in.

8) Touching or massaging a child in a sexual or sensual way.

9) Providing no sexual information or negative values about sex. Statements such as, "sex is dirty," telling off-color sexual jokes, and so forth can be hurtful. Not providing information on human sexuality and development, puberty, and appropriate values about sex can contribute to many unwanted outcomes. One would be that they will get the information somewhere. Indirectly, it implies there is something wrong with talking about it responsibly.

10) Lack of modeling of appropriate hugging or touching. This could be demonstrated by no display of affection as if it were taboo. The other extreme could be parents pressing the boundaries into what would be more appropriate displays of affection reserved for private

settings, such as passionate kisses, full body hugs with lots of physical stimulation and the adults fondling one another.

11) Exposing children to pornography.

12) Sensual looks that "undress" a child for the purposes of satisfying the offender's sexual fantasy.

13) Engaging the child in seductive, sensual dancing.

14) Ridiculing or embarrassing the child for having normal, healthy sexual feelings and responses.

15) Taking indecent liberties with a child. These could include:

a. snapping a bra strap or elastic band on underwear, pulling a bathing suit out enough to expose private areas,

b. slapping the child's buttocks

c. making indecent phone calls or texts (sexting).

16) Sexual innuendos, especially after the child has indicated for the perpetrator to stop or refrain. Even if a child who has been sexually abused makes sexual advances toward an adult, the adult's obligation is to set clear boundaries without shaming the child and proceed to guide the child into what is appropriate behavior.

5. Intellectual abuse.

Intellectual abuse involves examples of controlling and stifling the child by attacking, not allowing or ridiculing thoughts, the child's natural curiosity, and creative thinking. In the other extreme, parents may be inept, intellectually inadequate, or unaware of the importance of appreciating the intellect of a child. Intellectual stimulation may not be available for a variety of reasons. These parents could just be so selfishly embedded in their own lives to not notice or care to notice the intellectual needs of the children.

Parents could be lacking intellectual ability themselves or lack financial means to offer much in the way of intellectual stimulation. They could be so occupied with making a living that there would be no time for reading to a child or to listen to a school report the child has prepared. Sometimes it occurs that the child's intellectual ability is far superior to the parents or caregivers. As stated before, the primary caregivers may be simply repeating how they were raised and not be curious enough or brave enough to make any changes. This category can include the lack of guidance on how to problem solve life's inevitable dilemmas that arise.

Let it be noted that labeling a parent as intellectually abusive may be a somewhat gray area and difficult to define. An example would be when parents or primary caregivers are inadequate or unavailable while trying to make a living. So, the hurt would be situational. Again, the key to this determination has to come from the Survivor. Did the behavior hurt the Survivor?

6. Emotional abuse.

Emotional abuse can occur when a child is called degrading names, ridiculed, or experiences inconsistencies in the household rules. The child could be punished for changes in rules of which he or she might not have been made aware, such as if a parent is lax on one thing, then arbitrarily decides to be firm and punishing in that particular issue at some later time. This unexpected shift typically causes pain, anger and confusion. If children see emotionally laden things going on in the family, but are not allowed to talk about them, this can be emotionally painful. Worse yet is when caregivers deny or distort the child's reality. The adult might say something such as, "That is not what you saw or heard. You have it all wrong." The pain occurs when the child begins to question his or her own reality knowing at some level that he or she did know his or her truth about what was being experienced. As the child begins to deny or doubt his or her own truth, then a state of numbness tends to set in. The anger may come out at the time or later at parents and/or other authority figures. It could be pretty intense and seem irrational to the unaware observer.

Sometimes children are asked to be a part of family secrets. This is especially painful if a secret is kept from one spouse at the expense or exclusion of the other. A child or children may be expected to maintain silence and protect the secret. As noted before, this gives the child too much power in an area that should be left to the adults at the exclusion of the children. Children in the situation at some level know this is wrong. It becomes even more abusive if the content involves things to which children should not be exposed.

It is potentially abusive when the older generation or generations builds an unhealthy alliance with the child at the expense of the parent(s) or primary caregiver(s). Like before, as detailed in the section above on sexual abuse, this is incestuous in nature. Thus, this is emotionally abusive to the child. The child may be fooled into thinking he or she is special in one of these unbalanced, incestuous relationships, but in reality, he or she is being used at the child's expense.

I believe it is important for the reader to be exceptionally clear, if one is not already clear, on how to recognize incestuous relationships when they are occurring. "Incestuous" means the relationship has the dynamics that incest has. One who is an authority figure has access to a person under him or her. It could be a parent to a child, a grandparent to a grandchild, or a boss over an employee, a teacher over a student, a pastor over a parishioner, physician over a patient, or a government official over his or her constituents.

The second aspect of the incestuous relationship happens when the one in authority begins to use that access to take advantage of the one under him or her. It could begin seemingly innocent, such as the sharing of some private and personal feelings or experiences.

This might be presented as if others do not seem to understand the perpetrator. This is the seduction. Typically, it may lead to physical touching or, seemingly, again, "innocent" hugs. These then could lead to direct acts of sexual abuse.

I find Survivors may be more vulnerable even as adults to be lured into these incestuous encounters than the general population. Besides the high potential for someone to get hurt, I want the reader to understand the role anger plays in these situations. Let me refer to a couple examples of which we have been made aware through the media.

Our former President Clinton became sexually involved with a White House intern. An authority figure took advantage of a younger woman because he had access to her. Of course, she would be awestruck by receiving affectionate overtures by the most powerful man in the free world. His selfish, angry acts hurt his wife, his daughter, close friends, and every citizen in this country who cares to look into what happened.

But what I want the reader to be able to discern is the anger in this incestuous encounter. Being married, he was acting out anger at his marriage vows, indirectly implying that they had no value to him. He acted out his anger on the office he held and the trust given to him to run and guide this country with godly wisdom. He acted out his selfish anger onto the intern by turning her into a sex object for him to fondle and play with. I want to tread very lightly into the area of the victim's role because she has paid a heavy price for letting herself get involved in the sexual relationship. Like the purpose of this Guide, I hope she has been able to heal her wounds and have a fulfilling and rewarding life.

But I have been left with many unanswered questions for this young woman, as well as any other adult victim of an incestuous relationship. I fully understand how a child gets seduced or forced into an incestuous relationship, but what sets up the adult victim to not keep good boundaries when approached by an authority figure?

I believe the answer lies somewhere in the area of unresolved, repressed, or denied anger coupled with being fooled by the intrigue, the lure of going where one should not go. Were there boundary violations in one's past? There is enough anger being acted out on both sides, but what could be the source of it on the side of the victim? I will leave that for each victim to discover and work out as he or she uncovers his or her own truths. The real anger and related pain about a situation occurs when the victim comes face to face with the reality of how he/she was used and may have been fooled into believing at the time that he or she was "special" to the offender.

To conclude this discussion with other public examples, Tiger Woods fell to the same dynamic with his endless affairs. Ken Lay of Enron fame advising employees to continue investing in the company when he knew the house of cards it was built on was beginning to tumble down. In my view, he was acting out his anger selfishly onto those under him. I could go on and on with examples of public persons acting out their anger in an incestuous manner.

Affairs in the workplace are examples of people acting out the same dynamic. As stated before, it is incestuous if it is between a supervisor and an employee working under that supervisor. The one in the higher administrative role could be a department head, some officer, or even the CEO. Everybody gets hurt. There are no winners here except those who see the light, learn to deal with their anger to include the underlying pain, heal the wounds, and learn their lessons about the importance of protecting one's self by setting firm, healthy boundaries when necessary.

7. Family Violence.

This occurs when intense emotions between family members erupt into extremely loud yelling and screaming. These episodes can include physical punches, biting, and scratching intended to hurt another. Oftentimes, there are bruises, blackened eyes, and even broken bones as a consequence. These intense altercations typically evolve out of impasses in disagreements or as an attempt to express extreme displeasure with another's behavior. This way of handling disputes can be perpetrated onto non-family members too. The important distinction is that these episodes occur in the home or on the home property.

These events tend to leave the child observing these feeling terrified. Home is no longer a safe place or a sanctuary. It is not unusual that either the child gets struck just by being in the vicinity of the altercation or he or she can be the object of the rage. In some families, this is the way disputes are generally handled. It is not unusual for this to have been the preferred way across several generations. Thus, to these family members, this is considered normal.

This dynamic can be how a marital pair expresses their frustration with one another or by one dominating him- or herself over the other. If the child observes his or her mother getting battered, the emotional conflict this sets in motion can literally be incapacitating.

These episodes could be in the context of drunken behavior when a family member is a "mean drunk." Untreated alcoholism or drug use can be contributing factors in these families. The point is that directly or indirectly it hurts children who are in the presence of these violent expressions of rage. The emotional and physical toll can be enormous. It makes it difficult to enjoy family events and meals let alone the results of interrupted sleep patterns. If there are any tensions in the family, the child will feel it. This leaves the child feeling anxious and afraid as he or she wonders when will the next war break out. It is not unusual for children in these settings to be sick more often than other children. Life in these families can be likened to living in a combat war zone.

8. Spiritual abuse.

Spiritual abuse can come at the hands of spiritual leaders or workers in the church. These people may have carried out one or more of the abuses detailed above. The complication is often that the Survivor then wants nothing to do with church or rejects anything that rings of religion. Some people even go more extreme and turn to devil worship, the occult, or witchcraft. The other path a Survivor may take is to become enmeshed with the abusive authority figure and be available to do whatever this authority figure suggests or believes to be true. I expand on this concept below.

This is not always true, but the great majority of Survivors I have worked with who have experienced abuse of any kind tend to display mistrust, antagonism, or open rebellion to other authority figures. This seems to be even truer if they had been abused by caregivers or close family members, especially if the abuses were extreme. So, this realization brings me to make the statement that all abuse listed above has the potential to leave the Survivor spiritually abused.

Let me share a personal example of spiritual abuse that occurred with my oldest son. He was attending a Sunday school class at the United Methodist Church in our neighborhood and that I attended. The class teacher was a close neighbor who had a son my son's age, and they were classmates and friends. As far as I knew, my son enjoyed the class. Then out of the clear, or so it seemed, he did not want to go anymore. He became almost belligerent about it. When asked, he would not offer much. Not to be forcing religion on him, I did not push the issue. My son was eleven or twelve at the time. It was several years later that he revealed what had happened.

One day while he was visiting this family's home to play with the child his age, the father, the Sunday school teacher, got upset at something his son did. In anger, this father placed his hands around his son's neck and proceeded to pick him up while pushing him against the garage wall nearby. The father was shouting extremely angry words at his son. It was from that episode that my son decided that he did not want to go to that man's class anymore. I believe it was because of this episode that my son then lost all respect for organized religion and strongly resisted any encouragement to attend a church.

The other path the Survivor can go is to be bonded to or enmeshed with their offender(s) and do whatever to please him, her, or them, even if it is destructive to him- or herself. This all is an effort by the Survivor to be accepted by the offender coupled with the desire to avoid being hurt again. The other twist on this could be when the Survivor is carrying toxic shame that leads him or her to think of him- or herself as some form of damaged goods. Thus, his or her attempt to please the offender even when it might be harmful, can be driven by the desire to get back into the good graces of and be accepted by the offender. The final goal may then to be "whole" and "acceptable" again.

It is at the very core of the twelve-step program to use the phrase "Higher Power" in their first step and in their literature. The reality is that in alcoholic families or families with other addictions, children have typically seen, heard, and felt the hurts by the addicts or those who enable the addicts. Consequently, the possibility for spiritual abuse is highly likely. So, the twelve-step program gives permission to accept the new member's definition of their "Higher Power" however he or she wishes to define that for himself or herself.

The new member could choose to worship a tree. The rational is not to cut off the new member from the benefits of what the program offers by turning them off from insisting they call their "Higher Power" God, the God of Abraham, Isaac, and Jacob in the Bible. There are more Christian-based programs especially for those who do not have difficulty calling their higher power God.

It is interesting and powerful to note what Jesus said about protecting children from offenders as recorded in the New Testament, Matt 18:6, "But whoever causes one of these little ones who believe in me to sin, it would be better for him if a mill stone were hung around his neck, and he were drowned in the depth of the sea." This chapter in Matthew begins with Jesus' answer to the question about who is the greatest in the kingdom of heaven. To paraphrase the answer, it is to humble oneself like the child that Jesus had pulled over to himself.

The reader may or may not be aware that the twelve-step program is not only around the world as a powerful resource for recovering alcoholics and drug addicts but has extended into self-help programs for a multitude of other addictions or compulsive and problematic behaviors. Anonymous groups offer hope for over eaters, over-spenders, and bad check writers, just to name a few. All meetings are anonymous and led and attended by members who are not there to tell someone else what to do. Those attending are there to share the strength and hope of his or her own story of recovery. Each share what has worked for him or her. As stated above, it is not a perfect program because it is created by imperfect humans. It and other self-help programs modeled after it can be a great resource of recovery from addictions and compulsions of every description. These meetings are basically free.

9. Exposure to weird, bizarre, extreme if not violent events.

Some Survivors have been exposed to weird, bizarre, and extreme, if not violent, events. These are sometimes the very situations in which people slip off into different personalities and become someone else. Diagnostically, this splitting off or creating another personality is referred to as a Multiple Personality Disorder as a complication when sorting out one's feelings and triggers. This process is another creative way for the victim to survive. Bestiality is included in this category of abuse. These Survivors may have witnessed murders, body mutilations, animal or human sacrifices, or blood-drinking rituals, just to give you an idea of the kinds of things those who develop severe symptoms and diagnoses have been exposed to. Generally, the more horrific trauma events one was exposed to seem to correlate with the number of personalities created. If the Survivors do not create new personalities, they oftentimes have complex and severe psychiatric and psychological issues.

I have worked with those who have suffered horrendous trauma and for some reason did not split off other personalities. These seemed to consistently report that someone in the midst of the trauma let them know they were loved. For those, Adverse Childhood Events (ACE's) mention some of the kinds of situations that have been reported and of which I assisted directly or indirectly in their recovery. In one case, the physical and sexual abuse was awful. One young man as a child had things stuck in his rectum, ears, and mouth by a raging, brutal father. He had been sodomized by several men in his family. As an adult, he was an alcoholic, severe drug addict, sex addict, and had been diagnosed as having Depression and Attention Deficit/Hyperactivity Disorder.

If you were in his presence early on, he would be tapping with his fingers consistently as a way for him to cope with life moment to moment. He would not look at you directly, only from the side at an angle. It took many years for him to reach a healthy recovery. As with many alcohol or drug-addicted Survivors, he had to get sober first. Then and only then could he have a successful chance to benefit from the tasks as suggested in this Guide. His greatest fear was that he would grow old and not be attractive or appealing to a good woman. The extension of this fear was that he would miss the opportunity to have and raise a family. Later on, into his recovery, my primary job was to help him to set healthy boundaries that would allow him to develop relationships with appropriate partners. Without these boundaries, he tended to connect with other female, heterosexual sex and drug addicts. I continued to encourage him to get involved in a nurturing, healthy church and then be patient. He held his stand to seek a woman who was a committed member of a church since he desired a woman deeply committed to her faith. He did just that. Eventually, he met a perfect woman for him who had come to his church doing missionary work for the church as her parents before her had done. They dated and eventually married. They had their first child about a year ago. The last time I checked, things were going well for him and his new family.

Another case involved a woman whose family had been in a cult. She was taken to meetings and offered as a sexual sacrifice. She saw human bodies dismembered and body parts burnt in sacrifices. I said many times to her that it was amazing why she did not have multiple personalities. In her case, she had a very understanding grandmother who let her know she loved her and was fully aware of what was going on. The grandmother told her that when she thought the granddaughter could handle things without her, she would break her silence and confront the cult leaders. The grandmother knew when she did, she would be killed. The grandmother prepared the Survivor for this. The grandmother did break her silence and was later killed. It was a bumpy road to recovery, but this woman did eventually get some peace in her life.

As mentioned earlier, there was the case of a parent reading Bible verses about cautioning against sparring the rod of correction (Prov. 22:15 and Prov. 23:13,14). Some offenders interpret these verses literally, word for word, as justification for beating children into submission. The Bible also presents a caution to the offender (Matt. 18:3,4). Jesus honors children as being a model of humility and said if an offender causes a child who believes in Jesus to sin, it would be better if he had a millstone hung around his neck and then dropped into the depths of the sea.

To Bring This Segment to a Close

To bring this segment to a close, abuse perpetrated onto children is more prevalent than any of us would like to know. Because we share in the collective responsibility to protect children, it hurts us all when children are hurt needlessly. By doing this work of undoing the impact of abuse in your life or, as a Helper in someone else's life, we together are becoming a stronger voice to stand against these wrongs. Equally true, we become more viable advocates for protecting children.

I find it curious that as I am writing this, on the news it is being reported that more victims of an assistant football coach of a major university are stepping up to tell their stories of sexual abuse they claim was perpetrated by this man onto them. His denial of any wrongs he has done has apparently stirred the Survivors' anger and they are not going to be abused again. They are planning to testify in court. This is a great example of the use of healthy anger, which gives us the strength to press through circumstances when facing adversity.

Homework Assignment

Transfer any notes you have made as you read about the kinds of abuse that happened to you to the Worksheets for Recording Notes about Memories of Abuse. It is advisable for you to keep a separate journal of your recovery activities.

As you recall and record details of events, more details will come. Therefore, you will find it helpful to go back to what you already recorded, such as the example I mentioned above about "Uncle Mike's cabin. He touched me." You might revisit an entry like that several times as you recall more details. Proceed with writing your recollections on the Worksheets.

Go through each of these categories as many times as you need to ensure you get all the details of what happened to you.

Appendix D
Worksheets for Recording Notes from Reading Expanded Description of Types of Abuse

Using the results from the Outreach Response Survey in Appendix B, record detailed information about the type of Abuse that happened.

1. Neglect

   _____

   _____

   _____

   _____

2. Abandonment

   _____

   _____

   _____

   _____

3. Physical abuse

   _____

   _____

   _____

4. Sexual Abuse

   a. Direct_____

      _____

      _____

      _____

   b. Indirect_____

      _____

      _____

      _____

5. Intellectual Abuse

      _____

      _____

      _____

6. Emotional Abuse

      _____

      _____

      _____

7. Family Violence

      _____

      _____

      _____

8. Spiritual Abuse

_____

_____

_____

9. Bizarre and Extreme Events

_____

_____

_____

Appendix E
Master List of Abusive Events: A Review of the Hurtful Events

Master List of Hurtful Events:

For <u>each</u> of the Hurtful Events that occurred to the Survivor (recorded in Appendix B) answer the following questions:

(Make copies of these pages if needed):

1. Event # with Brief Descriptions as Reference to which Event

    _____

    _____

2. What Happened (Brief overview or summary)

    _____

    _____

    _____

3. How I was Hurt/Type of Abuse

    _____

    _____

4. Where This Happened (location, city, building(s), room(s), vehicle(s), out-of-doors, and so forth)

    _____

    _____

5. My Offender(s)

_____

6. My Age:

_____

7. When Did This Happen? (year, time of year, grade in school, season, temperature, and so forth)

_____

_____

8. Feelings I Had at the Time

_____

_____

9. What I Did with My Feelings

_____

_____

10. What I Learned about Myself

_____

_____

11. What I Learned about Relationships and Life in My Family

_____

_____

12. What I Learned about My Future

_____

_____

13. What I Wanted/Needed and Did Not Get

_____

_____

14. What I Lost/Was Taken from Me That I Want Back

_____

_____

15. What I Have Been Carrying That Does Not Belong to Me

_____

_____

16. What I Took Forward into My Future

_____

_____

17. The Cost

_____

_____

Appendix F
Helpful Statements, Affirmations and Positive Self-Talk to Review

1. To live a life in recovery is priceless.

2. I have a right to experience peace, fulfillment and to be living in my purpose for life.

3. Recovery comes one step at a time. The interesting thing is that the work remains there for us as we are ready.

4. I accept today that I take full responsibility for my part, what I did with what I was presented and making changes I need to make are mine too.

5. I accept today that there are no shortcuts to get into and keep a good recovery.

6. There are no shortcuts around this process of recovery.

7. I am willing to be totally honest about what happened, about how I survived, to include the ways I tried to medicate the pain.

8. Recovery begins in earnest when we each are willing to be honest about what happened, about what we each did with the event or events including the ways we tried to "medicate" the pain.

9. Carried shame is the result of an adult acting out his or her own shameful behavior at or in the presence of a child and taking no responsibility for the impact. Today, I let go of the shame I have been carrying. It does not belong in my body any longer.

10. I am aware that the greater degree that one has been hiding from the reality of the early hurtful events and their

impact, the more intense and severe the circumstances have to be to break one out of this hiding place.

11. I open the door today to new learnings and new beginnings.

12. To the question: "Am I willing to do whatever it takes?" I say an emphatic, "Yes."

13. I am willing to put the old ways aside and turn my life over to my higher power.

14. The price to get into a good recovery is nothing when compared to the cost to an unrecovered life.

15. I am committed to ignoring the set ups from the past and choosing to live life in the present.

16. When a Survivor begins to say he or she does not have the answers and his or her ways are not working, the Survivor now has a chance to get into the initial stages of recovery.

17. I can claim today that my feelings are mine. They reflect my reality and maybe most importantly, they are not up for debate!

18. To learn what one must learn, one has to stop the acting in or out or both, stop medicating, stop keeping secrets and to begin to take responsibility for what is really happening.

19. New hope begins when a Survivor claims: "I can't stand the pain any longer," or "There must be a better way," or "I cannot figure this out on my own any longer" or "My way is not working." This is a claim of powerlessness.

20. I am willing to ask at any moment: "How much is this about me and my past or you and your past?"

21. I am becoming aware of how extreme my behavior used to be. I did not have a clue, but others did and tried to tell me.

22. Serious recovery begins when I have been willing to be brutally honest about what happened, to be equally transparent about how I coped with it or the traumatic events, to be equally honest about how he or she is still being impacted, and finally and maybe more importantly, to be willing to let the old ways die and replace them with constructive, healthy, and more effective ways of living.

23. I choose to live in moderation.

24. However long it takes to get it, recovery is worth every effort to get there.

25. Feelings are our internal reference that we are alive and give us clues about what we are experiencing. To have your full range of feelings available from high highs to sad and painful lows and every step in between is what life is all about.

26. Some of us used to be hyper vigilant trying to discover clues in the present that might indicate the earlier trauma might be repeating.

27. "World, here I am imperfect at best just striving to make progress and trying to be a blessing."

28. To want different outcomes for my life I have no choice but to begin doing things differently. It is essential for change to take place.

29. Out of chaos comes clarity.

30. Today I take one step at a time and trust the process.

31. The point is that present-time events may have imbedded in them similar elements of the earlier traumatic event(s). Frequently, these previous elements may trigger a

response today that might have come out of my past and I react as if I were back in time. Knowing this is progress.

32. I believe today that healing is a process of giving tools for the conscious mind to have an active role again.

33. The healing I seek is about empowering the conscious mind to know what to do as well as retraining the subconscious to recognize and separate out current time realities from those in the past.

34. I can ask this question today: "How much of what I am feeling belongs to someone else and does not belong to me."

35. It becomes clear why some who are numb, filled with intense emotions, or are depressed, tend to develop drug and alcohol addictions or other obsessions and compulsions such as gambling, acting out sexually, overeating and engaging in other high-risk behaviors. This list could go on and on. These behaviors in the context of surviving trauma have been referred to as ways of "self-medicating."

36. It becomes a time for celebration when a Survivor faces "old" triggers and stays in present time reality to cope effectively with them by not dissociating or acting them out or inwardly in some way without conscious awareness as used to occur previously in my unrecovered state.

37. I enjoy reminding myself that children have a right to be protected, to be safe, to play, to learn, to love and be loved. Part of growing up is to experience forgiving and being forgiven too. They have a right to be curious, to make mistakes and be taught and guided.

38. The Survivor is the final authority on whether an act is abusive or not.

39. Over time as I am becoming skilled at knowing my feelings and thoughts, it is almost second nature for me to speak about them to others as appropriate.

40. I am increasingly aware of how many rarely or sometimes never claim their feelings clearly and openly. They typically embed them in voice tones or in other non-verbal ways. To them I can say inside, "Oh well. They will have to discover the benefits of expressing one's feelings clearly on their own. All I can do is continue to be a model for the healthy expression of feelings."

41. I did not cause the act(s) of abuse. I was an innocent child deserving to be protected.

42. Take it one step at a time and trust the process.

43. In some way, only known to each individual, it all starts making sense.

44. Children have a right to be protected.

45. I was hurt but I am not broken. What was done to me or in my presence was wrong, but I am on my way to being free of the impact.

46. From the moment the first abuse happens, I was then both a victim and a Survivor.

47. Today, I take time to feel, note what is happening as the wave of feelings come, and talk only after the wave has passed.

48. This is my recovery, and the work will remain there for me to do as I am prepared to move ahead.

49. Because we share in the collective responsibility to protect children, it hurts us all when children are hurt needlessly. By doing this work of undoing the impact of abuse in your life or, as a Helper in someone else's life, we together are becoming a stronger voice to stand against these wrongs.

50. So, this realization brings me to make the statement that all abuse has the potential to leave the Survivor spiritually abused.

51. As we each become free of the impact of abuse, we become more viable advocates for protecting children.

52. The most loving thing you can do is to affirm the Survivor's reality. You can say things such as, "What happened to you was terrible. No child should have had to go through that," or, "You were a child. I am so sorry that you had to see/hear/feel what you did." To listen and accept his or her truth is the most loving and healing thing you can do.

53. By completing the work of bringing these painful, abusive acts out into the light, these brave acts will encourage others to follow our lead to personal freedom.

54. Through the visualization process of watching a scene and answering the questions that followed, I became incredibly clear and specific about what happened to me.

55. I believe there is hope in knowing there was a time when I was curious, loving, enjoyed being myself, and could be totally engrossed in playing, maybe happy pulling at my own toes or falling backwards watching a bird fly overhead.

56. There was a time in my young life before the abuse started when I was whole. I was free to just be that precious child I was meant to be.

57. Having gone through reliving the abusive history, one has to ask how anyone could let themselves bring harm to such a precious child. It is healthy to be angry about that reality.

58. So, I accept this work is about building bridges from my new past and making it a part of my life today and into the future.

59. I know that eventually, the availability of my new learnings will become embedded in my thinking and actions without much conscious effort.

60. This is time to give myself lots of permission to be me and to celebrate being me today.

61. This is my new life. No one can take it from me. It is mine to treasure, protect, and to build on.

62. This is my life and my recovery. I have the right to have my feelings, my dreams, my joys, my relationships, my rewards, and my achievements. I am unwilling to let anyone take my recovery from me.

63. The best way to know that I am on the right track involves identifying what my choices are.

64. I am excited to know that I can rehearse events coming up in the future.

65. Today I stand my ground when I need to.

66. What I notice as I move into the rehearsed scene in real time is that I tend to be more likely to act out the version I practiced.

67. I find comfort in knowing there will come a time when I will act on this new learning without any rehearsal.

68. Being aware of my choices is the best way to know that I am in charge of my responses.

69. I am comforted as I am reminded that I am not a victim of the ways I used before to just survive. I am the parent of my life now.

70. The greatest gift to others is to be able to pass it on. Just maybe I might find myself being a guide, a Helper, for another Survivor. What a treasure that would be!

71. I can now say with confidence from personal experience that recovery is not an easy process. But it is worth working through, step by step. There are no shortcuts to personal freedom.

72. The world is a better place now because of what I have done through this program. I can now claim I am a recovering Survivor and proud of it!

Appendix G
Self-Relaxation

There are many uses of your internal tool called, imagination. It is used to conceive future achievements, to practice new behaviors, to "see" images in the clouds or to check if a word "looks correct" for spelling. It is used extensively in trauma recovery treatment from reviewing the details of disturbing scenes, to re-writing painful memories, forgiving offenders as well as forgiving one's self. The so-called internal screen in our mind's eye has a multitude of applications. One of them detailed below will assist you in achieving a wonderful state of total relaxation in 60 seconds or less with practice. This relaxation exercise is best used when preparing yourself for getting the most from closing your eyes and "going inside to access your mind's eye."

I invite you to follow the instructions listed below to achieve a peaceful state of relaxation. Read through the list (1-21) to get familiar with the sequence and the body parts to picture in your mind's eye. You will move from your feet up to your brain. Get comfortable where you are sitting because you will not be moving for the next few minutes. When you are ready, close your eyes and begin picturing the body part you will direct to relax. Close your eyes and follow these instructions:

1. In your mind's eye picture your feet and ankles. As you do, ask your feet and ankles to relax. Relax every muscle and tendon even your skin. Feel the tension and tightness leave your feet and ankles.

2. Now do the same thing with your lower legs. Picture them and tell every muscle and tendon to relax all the

way around and all the way through. Feel the tension and tightness leave.

3. Picture your knees and tell every muscle and tendon in your knees to relax all the way around and all the way through. Feel the tension and tightness leave.

4. Picture your thighs and tell every muscle and tendon to relax all the way around in your thighs. Feel the tension and tightness leave.

5. Picture your buttocks and tell every portion to relax all the way through. Feel the tension and tightness leave.

6. Picture your pelvic floor and tell every muscle and tendon to relax all the way through. Feel the tension and tightness leave.

7. Picture your abdomen and tell every muscle and tendon to relax all the way through. Feel the tension and tightness leave.

8. Picture your ribs and back all around and all the way through as you tell all your vital organs to keep functioning as normal and tell all the muscles and tendons around the back and ribs to relax and go limp as all the tension and tightness leave."

9. Picture your shoulder blades and tell all the muscles and tendons to relax as all the tension and tightness leave.

10. Picture your upper arms and tell all the muscles and tendons to relax as all the tension and tightness leave.

11. Picture your lower arms and tell all the muscles and tendons to relax as all the tension and tightness leave.

12. Picture your hands and tell all the muscles and tendons to relax as all the tension and tightness leave.

13. If you are sitting upright, using the least amount of energy, balance your head just right. Then ask the muscles and tendons around your neck to relax and feel the tension and tightness leave all the way around.

14. Now to the head, start with your jaws. Picture your jaws and tell them to relax and feel all tension and tightness leave.

15. Picture your temples and tell them to relax and feel all tension and tightness leave.

16. Picture the back of your head, along the top of your head to the top of your forehead and tell them to relax and feel all tension and tightness leave.

17. Picture your forehead and the areas around your cheeks, nose and mouth and tell them to relax and feel all tension and tightness leave.

18. Lastly, imagine your brain. Focus on it and ask it to relax and be still.

19. Now, take note as to what it is like being totally relaxed and at peace. Stay in this peaceful state as long as you like.

20. Open your eyes when you are ready.

21. Stand up and do some stretches. You have been still for a few minutes. Before going on with your day, remind yourself you can return to this peaceful, relaxed state any time you wish. With repeated practice, you can achieve this relaxed state in about the time it takes to snap your fingers.

In closing, be aware, the more you practice this, the quicker you will get at achieving this totally relaxed state in less than 60 seconds. Also note, you take this skill with you anywhere you are. Enjoy!

Selected References

ACE Reporter. (2003.) Vol 1(1): 1-4. (A free research publication dealing with the effects of adverse childhood experiences on adult health and wellbeing.) http://www.acestudy.org/healthpubliletions/ACER eporter

Berkowitz, L. (1982.) "Adverse conditions as stimuli to aggression." *Advances in Experimental Social Psychology*, 15: pp. 249-288.

Brier, John and Hodges, Monica. (2010.) "Assessing the Effects of Early and Later Childhood Trauma in Adults." In (Eds.) Lanius, Ruth A; Vermetten, Eric and Pain, Carla. *Impact of Early Life Trauma on Health and Disease*. NY: Cambridge University Press.

Bright, J.I., Baker, K.D. and Neimeyer, R.A. (1999.) "Professional and Para-professional Group Treatments for Depression: A Comparison of Cognitive-behavioral and Mutual Support Interventions." *Journal of Consulting and Clinical Psychology*, 67, pp. 491-501.

Capacchione, Lucia. (1991.) *Recovery of Your Inner Child: The Highly Acclaimed Method of Liberating Your Inner Self*. New York: Simon & Schuster/Fireside.

Carkuff, Robert. (2008.) *The Art of Helping* (ninth edition). Amherst, MA: Possibilities Publishing.

Diagnostic and Statistical Manual of Mental Disorders, (fifth edition.) (DSM V). (2013.) Arlington, VA: American Psychiatric Association, American Psychiatric Publishing.

Driskell, J. E., Copper, C. and Morfan, A. (1994.) "Does Mental Practice Enhance Performance?" *Journal of Applied Psychology*, 79: pp. 481-492.

Dubner, Z.E. and Motta, R.W. (1999.) "Sexually and Physically Abused Foster Care Children and Posttraumatic Stress Disorder." *Journal of Consulting and Clinical Psychology*, 67(3): pp. 367-373.

Ehlers, A.S., Hackmann, A. and Michael, T. (2004.) "Intrusive Re-experiencing in Post-Traumatic Stress Disorder: Phenomenology, Theory and Therapy." *Memory*, 12(4): pp. 403-415.

Eysenbach; G., Powell, J., Englesakis, M., Rizo, C. and Stern, A. (2004.) Health Related Virtual Communities and Electronic Support Groups: Systematic Review of the Effects of Online

Falsetti, Sherry A., Monier, Jeannine and Resnick, Jeannine. (2005.) "Chapter 2: Intrusive Thoughts in Posttraumatic Stress Disorder." (Ed.) Clark, David A. *Intrusive Thoughts in Clinical Disorders, Theory, Research and Treatment*. New York City: Guilford Press, pp 40-41.

Fanning, Patrick. (1988.) *Visualization for a Change*. Oakland, CA: New Harbinger Publications, Inc. p.128.

"Former Foster Children in Oregon and Washington Suffer Posttraumatic Stress Disorder at Twice the Rate of U.S. War Veterans." (2005.) *Casey Family Programs*. Boston, MA: Harvard Medical School.

Gillem, Troy. (2013.) *Bipolar Battle Plan: Fighting the War Against Bipolar Disorder*. Bloomington, IN: iUniverse LLC.

Haber, Russell. 2002. "Virginia Satir: An Integrated Humanistic Approach." *Contemporary Family Therapy*, Vol 24(1) March: pp. 23-34.

Humphreys, K. (2004.) *Circles of Recovery: Self-help Organizations for Addictions*. Cambridge, England: Cambridge University Press.

Johnson, David R., Lahad, Modi and Gray, Amber. (2009.) "Creative Therapies for Adults." In (Eds.) Foe, Edna, Keane, Terence M., Friedman, Mathew J. and Cohen, Judith. *Effective Treatments for PTSD: Practical Guidelines from the International Society for Traumatic Stress Studies*. New York: Guilford Press. p 480.

Johnson, Jenny. (2012.) "Oprah: I was raped when I was only nine." *Irish Examiner*. November 28. https://www.irishexaminer.com/.

Kaufman, Gershen. (1996.) *Psychology of Shame: Theory and Treatment of Shame-based Syndromes*. (2nd Edition.) NY, NY: Springer Publishing Company.

Lanius, R.; Vermetten, E. and Pain, C. (Eds.) (2010.) *The Impact of Early Life Trauma on Health and Disease: The Hidden Epidemic*. Cambridge, England: Cambridge University Press.

Moos, R. and Timko, C. (2008.) "Outcome Research on Twelve Step and Other Self-help Programs." In (Eds.) Galanter, M and Kleber, H.D. *Textbook of Substance Abuse Treatment*. (4th Edition.) Washington, D.C.: American Psychiatric Press, pp. 511-521.

Peer to Peer Interaction." *British Medical Journal*, 328: pp. 11661170.

Price, Matt. (2014.) *Inner Child: Find Your True Self, Discover Your Inner Child and Embrace the Fun in Life*. Amazon. Redding, Carol A. (Ed). (2003.) *ACE Reporter*. April, vol. 1, (1).

Richardson, Alan. (1969.) *Mental Imagery*. New York: Springer Publishing Co.

Satir, V. and Baldwin, M. (1983.) *Step by Step: A Guide to Creating Change in Families*. Palo Alto, CA: Science and Behavior Books.

Sheikh, Aness A., Kerngendorf, Robert G. and Sheikh, Katherina S. (2003.) "Healing Images: Historical Perspective." In (Ed.) Sheikh, Aness, A. *Healing Images: The Role of Imagination in Health*. Amityville, NY: Baywood Publishing Company, Inc. pp. 3-26. Singer, J. (2005.) *Imagery in Psychotherapy*. Washington, D.C.: American Psychological Association.

Skelton K., Norrholm, S.D., Janovic, T. and Bradley-Davina, B. (2014.) "PTSD and Gene Variants: New Pathways and New Thinking." *Pharmacology*, 62:(2), pp. 628-637.

Taal, Jan and Krop, John. (2003.) "Imagery in the Treatment of Trauma." In (Ed.) Sheikh, Aness A. *Healing Images: The Role of Imagination in Health*. Amityville, NY: Baywood Publishing Company, Inc. pp. 396-407.

Taylor, Catherine L. (1991.) *The Inner Child Workbook: What to Do with Your Past When It Will Not Go Away*. New York: Penguin Putman, Inc.

Van der Kolk, Bessel A., M.D. (2014) *The Body Keeps the Score*. New York, New York: Penguin Books.

Weis, J.; Smucker, M. and Dresser, J. (2003.) "Imagery: Its History and Use in the Treatment of Posttraumatic Stress Disorder." In (Ed.) A. Sheikh. *Healing Images: The Role of Imagination in Health*. Amityville, New York: Baywood Publishing Company Inc. pp. 381-395.

Whitfield, Charles L., M.D. (2010.) *Healing the Inner Child*. Deerfield Beach, Florida: Health Communications.

Whitfield, Charles L., M.D. (1995.) *Memory and Abuse: Remembering and Healing the Wounds of Trauma*. Deerfield Beach, Florida: Health Communications.

Winnicott, D.W. (1965.) "Ego Distortions in Terms of True Self and False Self: The Maturation Process and Facilitative

Environment" *Studies in the Theory of Emotional Development.* NY: International Universities Press. pp. 140-157.

Note: For a more extensive list of selected references and selected references organized by topic, see: *Becoming Free: Recovering from Adverse Childhood Events (ACEs), (2017.)* by Gary J. Butler, Ph.D.

www.ingramcontent.com/pod-product-compliance
Lightning Source LLC
Chambersburg PA
CBHW060812120626
46557CB00001B/188